My Korea

A YEAR LOST IN SERVICE
1946-1947

JOHN BOWERS

Four Seasons Press, New York

Also by John Bowers

Fiction

> *The Colony*, 1971
> *No More Reunions*, 1973
> *Helene*, 1975
> *Love in Tennessee*, 2008

Collected Articles

> *The Golden Bower*s, 1972

Non-fiction

> *In the Land of Nyx*, 1984
> *Chickamauga and Chattanooga: The Battles*
> *   that Doomed the Confederacy*, 1994

Biography

> *Stonewall Jackson: Portrait of a Soldier*, 1989

For my sons,

Nick and David

Korean Peninsula

Historical Background

Once the Allied forces knew they were going to win the war in Europe, they turned their attention to the defeat of Japan, a formidable prospect given the fierce resistance of the Japanese and the increasing frequency of their kamikaze attacks. At the Yalta Conference of February 1945, attended by F.D.R., Stalin and Churchill, Stalin was persuaded to attack the Japanese forces in China, and the US would attack the Japanese from the Pacific. Prior to the Yalta Conference it had been agreed that once the Japanese were defeated, the USSR would accept the surrender of the Japanese north of the 38th parallel and the US would accept their surrender south of the 38th parallel. This is how US troops came to be occupying Korea in 1946.

The idea had been that a united Korea would soon be sufficiently rebuilt to stand on its own and would be granted independence. However, the political ideologies and economic aspirations of the two occupying nations were in opposition and cold war tensions were mounting worldwide. Finally, in June 1950, the US withdrew the last of its troops from South Korea whereupon, on 25 June 1950, North Korean forces attacked South Korean forces at the 38th parallel. Thus, began the Korean War.

Author's Note

In this account of a long ago and unforgettable period in the author's life, a few names have been changed or invented and a character or two are composites, but essentially it is the brutal truth, in all clarity, as far as the author could recall it.

My Korea
A Year Lost in Service 1946 - 47

One day early in my life I found myself on The Marine Dragon. It was a troopship and we were leaving San Francisco Bay at twilight and I stood on deck not quite sure what would happen next. I had never been on a ship or boat. I have never seen the ocean before. The ship sailed slowly and smoothly away, hardly a ripple felt from the sea. I imagined it would remain so until we reached a place called Korea that was out there somewhere, where my orders said I was heading. Its whereabouts if not significance lay beyond my grasp, out there somewhere or other halfway around the globe. I knew nothing of its history or what we were doing there – or cared to. I had joined the Regular Army and they would do with me what they wished – and they did. Later, I was promised, I could come home to the GI Bill and college. I wished I had been assigned to Japan, though. At least I'd heard of it. The embers of World War II still smoldered and I knew very well where Japan was and what it had done to deserve occupation. They had bombed Pearl Harbor and geisha girls were there. Oh, boy, I would have liked to have gone the other way, to Germany. It was a wreck but the remains of World War II were there. There were *frauleins*. They had a history I knew about, and they had lost the war and deserved to. It was an interesting place.

San Francisco's twinkling lights, the imposing Golden Gate, began to fade just as the ship began a barely perceptible undulation, an augury of much more to follow. I didn't know enough to be excited or afraid or anything. I had joined the Army immediately after high school, and I now stood on deck, among a clot of like-minded innocents, letting wind whip my face, feeling myself rise and fall as the ship began to rise and fall, and the United States disappeared.

Young Romans joined Tiberius's legions to march off to the Rhineland in much the same way. Jobless Munich drop outs put on Wehrmacht helmets and rode into Paris as occupiers. I didn't realize I was going over as an occupier myself. I didn't realize a lot of things. I was 18 and hardly needed to shave.

As darkness fell, I went below where bunks rose on top of one another. Dim lights shone and card games were going on and the click of dice sounded. I was agile then and climbed to a top bunk so no one was above me. I passed out as I heard someone whacking off under a blanket some rows away.

During the night I felt the ship roll left to right, or port to starboard, as I got to call it later when I forced myself to think about it. The motor went chug, chug, chug. I woke to the dim greenish light still on but no sounds of cards or dice. I swung over my berth and gravitated down to the hard metal floor that was weaving like a carnival's Fun House where normal surroundings no longer existed. I made my way to, what I came to call, the Head: a line of sinks with mirrors above; a row of tin commodes where water continually gushed in each one. You didn't have to flush. It was done for you.

I had caught a terrible cold in Camp Stoneman before departure but I forgot about it. This was one sure way to get rid of a cold. I was propelled to a bowl where water gushed and began throwing up. I didn't plan or think about it. I didn't have time. I was just there, eventually on my hands and knees, puking. It was not just once and then relief. It kept going on and on. Others now came in and before long the bowls were all taken. I saw out of the corner of my eye someone from my hometown – we'd joined up together – and he started to laugh at me and then puked and staggered out. I think I stayed on my hands and knees for three days and nights. It felt like it. I couldn't stand. I didn't want to.

My body, my whole spirit, said to keep puking. I heard, among the few words that passed above me, that we were passing the Aleutians and had been hit by a tidal wave. I didn't care. I could die for all I cared. I kept puking until finally only green bile came up. Over the Squawk Box came announcements, those to report for KP or roll call or if somebody was still alive. Fantastically, I heard: "Now hear this. Now hear this. Private John Bowers, RA14218267, report to Hatch 3 for deck duty. If you are not there by 1300 you will be counted AWOL." Did they think I'd gone overboard? They could come lasso me. They could hold me up and shoot me. My head stayed over the bowl. Would it ever end? I heard someone say, "It's not over until you can taste your asshole coming up."

Water gushed from the tin commode, sprinkling me with drops. On the enameled ship's wall near me, in neat lettering, someone had written, "I have shit on the banks of the Wabash, I have shit over Niagara Falls, but this is the first time I've sat down to shit and at the same time watered my balls." The Army! The Marine Dragon had had service in World War II. It had ferreted troops to the Philippines and Guadalcanal and God knows where else when the world was almost being blown apart. I was on it just after that. Who had had the inspiration, the ability to get into a position, and felt the necessity, to pen it? Someone else, in a nearby script, had scrawled, "If a Texan's brains were as big as his balls, there'd be no writing on the shit house walls." Out of the Army, in my 20's I read all of T.S. Eliot. I read Shakespeare over and over again. I remember scattered lines, "I should have been a pair of ragged claws, scuttling across the floor of silent seas." Why is it now, so many decades later, as memories fade into the sunset, that I remember more clearly those lines on the Marine Dragon and what the script looked like than anything from Wallace Stevens? It means I believe that here was the moment that I realized I had left Tennessee and the assurance of a clean warm bed and meals on time and was sailing into the future.

* * *

I lie in my top berth, climbing up I don't know how, every few minutes leaning over to go through the motions of heaving when nothing comes up. They call it the "dry heaves." The good old Marine Dragon bow goes under and the stern comes out. And the propeller goes slap slap slap against the water, shaking the ship like the start of an earthquake. The ship kneels far far to port, far far to starboard and why it doesn't turn upside down I don't know and then uprights itself with a jolt. Over the Squawk Box comes, "Now here this, hear this…" I recognize no names called for duty. My name is forgotten. There is never a news flash, nothing about a tidal wave or where we are or where we might end up. Sometimes there is an order not to venture topside as if anyone in his right mind wanted to adventure up there. I am not in my right mind. I don't care if I live or die. Three months before I was on my high school tennis team and was in love with a girl I had never kissed. At home we either had fried chicken or beaten steak every night for supper since the day I was born. "Now hear this, now hear this…"

I notice eventually that there is movement down below in the aisle. It could be a day or two later, even a week, but I realized that soldiers were moving out, on the way to the mess hall for food or topside for air. I was happy to see activity, people alive and doing something. I thought I should at least try to force something down. What awaited me was steam, rancid odor, and silverware banging down and rattling on trays and a few comrades who were in no hurry to go through the chow line. The food is something greenish yellow and looking rubbery. I gag and turn around. I put on a bulky life preserver that is required for going topside and I'm up there at last and it's early morning. Impressive white crested waves begin in the distance and head for the ship. When they arrive the ship rises high and falls deep and then holds for a moment of calm. All that keeps one from going overboard is a thin railing and a chain drawn between two stanchions. I stand a few feet back in my life preserver and fight to keep my balance. How long would I be able to float if I slip over the edge? Would they reverse course and come get me or would they notice? Would I be written up in the hometown paper? While thinking I see this old guy in glasses heave. He could have been all of thirty. It goes out straight, an unbroken yard or two, flying over the railing. I see that now his cheeks are shrunken and he has a look of deep despair. "I just lost my teeth," he says.

Popping up at my side is a long-time buddy from my Tennessee hometown, the one who saw me heaving the first morning in the Head. We joined the Army together along with three other hometown boys and managed to get assigned together, to basic training at Ft. Knox and to overseas. He is called "Daffy" because his last name is "Ducker." He is 18, too, and already losing his hair. He continually looks at my full head of hair and curses. He took the girl of my dreams away from me in high school, the one I'd never kissed, and regularly back then reported how far he has gotten with her. He claimed to have rubbed her stomach. Where exactly that was on her anatomy he did not go into. I didn't ask. Back home he lived with an extended family member down the block, his father handsome but absent and a near do well and said to be a drunk. A rambling man. His mother, still in love with him, turned over the money Daffy trustingly sent to put in a savings account. Now on deck, as the ship rises and falls, he exaggerates the motion, going up on his toes with "whoo-eee" and down with "ooh-eee." "Stop it," I say, and he does so with an infuriating chuckle. Then he does it again more slowly. I could kill him. But he is hometown with all its associations and I am comforted with his maddening presence. Others aboard present a different and mystifying picture. It is the geography of America. Only in the Army would you find such a collection under one roof – a Brooklyn Jew, a Dakota Scandinavian, a New Jersey Greek, slow quiet homesick Southerners, violent Southerners, superior-acting Northerners who bitch but can't put up a pup tent, Westerners who wrangled horses and can be counted on to injure themselves attempting some harebrain feat. Many I recognize from Basic Training. We are all holed up, heading for Korea in the fall of 1946.

*   *   *

One soldier who would crop up in various guises during my tour in the Hermit Kingdom was Private First Class Aberdeen. Somehow I took it that this wasn't his real name although I had no proof. To me Aberdeen was an Army base like Fort Knox. He regularly inserted himself into any group or conversation that came within shouting distance. Some of us might be talking quietly about hometown girls or movie actresses, even a sister, and he'd say, although no one asked him, "I got me some cuzzy back in Stoneman, A nurse. She let me play stink finger when I was laid up with the croup." Why didn't he say, pussy? You had to imagine what "stink finger" meant. He didn't seem to have any regional base or ethnic source. He was of average height and average looks and nothing about him evoked leadership. Yet he kept cropping up, on the Marine Dragon and later when we landed at Inchon, an influence on all that happened around him. Aberdeen.

*   *   *

A day or two after we had sailed past the Aleutians, the ship fell into steady, plodding thrust. No more rolling, port to starboard, no more the propeller rising above the water and shaking the craft like a dog coming out of the water. The sea had minimal slow-moving waves and we could stand on deck at twilight, out in the air, and escape from the clouds of tobacco smoke, the racket of gambling, and the stench of unwashed bodies. No land or boat seen anywhere. And one and all below deck became ravenously hungry. There still was little line up for the yellowish green glop that was slung on the metal tray in the chow line. No more sex fantasies skittering across the brain. Now I dreamed, awake and asleep, of food. I played back coming in my warm quiet kitchen back home and sinking my teeth into a peanut butter sandwich. How soft it felt, followed by a bite of a hard apple and a swig of milk. Why hadn't I ever prized that ordinary moment as one of the greatest things in life? I thought of the shaft of sunlight coming through the kitchen window back home, the hum of the refrigerator, the sparkle of the plate on which the sandwich lay. The kitchen was warm. Oh, how I thought of that sandwich – and fried chicken, chicken and dumplings, and skillet cornbread slathered with butter. I could cry. I knew hunger. For the first time in my life I knew hunger that offered no relief.

And some of us became obsessed with the idea that the billeted officers, and certainly the Merchant Marines that ran the ship, were eating like kings. It figured. It was then that a plan was drawn up. We would send out a patrol to break into officer storage and see what food we could steal. It was drawn up like a military operation with volunteers recruited. I did not join, didn't even think about it, since once volunteering for the Army had been enough and I told myself I would never volunteer again, for anything. But I witnessed the patrol being formed and was curious. I noted that Aberdeen was in the thick of it as were several veterans of WWII who had re-upped for benefits and now found themselves deep in the Pacific. They went off in a half crouch, looking left and right, scurrying up iron steps into officer territory. Small waves lashed the ship. Down below deck, from the Enlisted Men's mess, came banging kitchen sounds and muted talk. An acrid smell of the inedible followed. Above, there was a long silence from where the patrol had disappeared, then a yelp, and then they came flying down the steps followed by a Merchant Marine screaming, "Halt!"

Who would ever stop for a Merchant Marine? Later we heard stories. From Private First Class Aberdeen: "They got a big padlock on their food locker. Oh, they know, they know! Them sons a bitches!"

From another, "They sleep four or five to a state room. Can you believe it?"

I dreamed about being an officer. I would return home with gold bars on my shoulders. Going overseas I would lie on my back in pajamas reading books from light that came from a port hole. Right now I was starving. Later scuttlebutt had it that a Procurement Officer had grafted money meant for the Enlisted Men's Mess and went to jail for it. I didn't know whether to believe it or not but it sounded reasonable.

One early evening, just after Enlisted Men's chow time, at which few showed up, three Merchant Marine cooks popped up on deck carrying platters of fried chicken. I see those chicken parts rise now on the plates, three or four rows deep. Perhaps the Merchants had felt sorry for us and wanted to give us a treat from their own Mess, perhaps their spirit was altruistic, but when we on deck inhaled the aroma and saw the goods, the plates carried forth, a riot broke out. Seeing the troops race toward them, the Merchants flung one plate after another onto the bare deck. That's all they could do to save themselves. The deck was wet and slippery and the grease from the chicken made it even more so. We scampered and fought like animals for a piece but I was not lucky or aggressive enough, so I watched others grab and gnaw and go back for more. I came close, though. At first the Merchants had perhaps flung the chicken out of self-defense but then made a game of it, laughing as they made turns like a bull fighter, flinging the chicken away at the last second and watching the troops rush past within inches. The last plate empty, they disappeared.

Life on board became what I imagined prison to be. We gritted our teeth to get through it. Each day lived through it was a victory. We found ways to lighten the load. Some gambled. I found a supply of paperbacks produced a short time before during World War II. They came in rectangular shapes on thin paper. Everything from WWII was on thin rations. I left alone any tome that required energy or the pursuit of knowledge or self-improvement. I picked up "The Voice of the Turtle" by John Van Druten. It was a play, but it would do. I liked the blurb on the cover, something about a soldier on leave in Manhattan who calls on a girl in her apartment in Manhattan. I took it and retired to my berth. *Now hear this, now hear this …* and bunch of names crackled over the squawk box to report for KP immediately, mine not among them. They must have forgotten about me.

I sank into "The Voice of the Turtle" as if into a warm bath. I felt happy, a feeling I had forgotten about. I felt soothed and calm and optimistic as I turned page after page. I forgot ship and soldiering and a dice game a few berths down. What got to me was the romance of this play. A woman named Sally Page had just gotten over a bad affair and this soldier appears on her doorstep out of the blue. It moves slowly and tantalizingly, some misunderstanding and conflict along the way, and at the end they make their way to bed, she's forgotten about the bad affair and the soldier has a place to stay for the night. Simple, but it had everything. It had a feel for what kind of things happened in New York, a sense that no matter how dislocated and bereft someone becomes there the gates can open unrepentantly to wonderland. Miraculous things can happen.

We told our own stories top-side to temporary buddies. Burden was from somewhere up North. He had bad teeth and a crooked smile. He had slept in the bunk next to me at Basic Training at Ft. Knox and I enjoyed his company. He told about packages he was going to get from home once we got to Korea – salamis and cheeses by the carload. He told about meals his mother placed on the table back home. He came from a Slavic family and his name was shortened from a longer one with a "ski" at the end. His mother conjured up images of exotic and mouth watering dishes. "Momma Burden is really going to feed us," I said. I noticed him ducking his head at this as if he was already guarding the riches that would arrive.

He told me about a sister who did not seem all that bright. Actually Burden was not all that bright himself. It was one reason I liked him. I could relax around him. I didn't have to strain myself. One fascinating thing about him was that he slept with one eye half open. I would speak to him as he lay with that one eye half-open, staring at me, and it took me a while to realize that he wasn't looking at me but was asleep. He snored in a sort of whinny. He didn't read, he didn't talk about movies or what was happening in the world. He mentioned no girlfriend. He laughed without really opening his mouth, something hard to do. He just nodded and shook his shoulders. There wasn't much to laugh about on board, though. "Oh, the fucking Army," he said. He bitched, as we all did, about everything connected with the Army and the ship and he stared morosely at the water that spread out against the sky. "Fucking ship," he said. I don't think he knew its name.

After a pause and into the silence, he said, "Your brother wasn't a football star. That's a bunch of crap. Your family don't sit around reading books."

It was like a slap. Had I been bragging? Had I been setting myself up as select and privileged? Probably.

Undoubtedly. But I had left out a lot in telling him my story (we all told each other our stories out of boredom.) I just wanted to be back home while the Marine Dragon chugged onward and below deck the troops cursed and shot dice. I left out in my broadcasting about a book-lined home that we didn't have a car when nearly everyone else did in town. I left out that I was ashamed to bring a new buddy home from Junior High for lunch once. He lived in a huge red brick home with sparkling white trim. Paint was peeling from our old gray frame home. In my mind I always left out that his parents were divorced, a really startling thing back then, and the big brick home belonged to his doctor uncle, his mother's brother, not to his father. His father had taken to drink and I didn't know what to think about that. All I could think about was the exterior of a home, never what went on inside it. It was the outward show of a thing that mattered, never the myriad concealments within.

Actually, I joined up in large part to wear a uniform, to show the world that I was acceptable, that people would immediately recognize me as someone who had passed the test. The uniform spoke for me. I didn't have to say a word. My older brother by 12 years had worn a white naval officer's uniform in the War, and that had really spoken loudly. Before that, his football and basketball uniforms, his name in the papers, hadn't exactly spoken in a whisper. They made me want to put on a United States uniform myself. And to seek out Adventure, to go off into foreign places, far from the streets of my small town in East Tennessee.

After Basic Training at Fort Knox I had had the chance to become cadre, a drill master for incoming recruits, where I had been miserable a little while before myself. I was offered the position because I had led my Company from Basic before hundreds on the Fort Knox drill field, a general in the stands, because I had somehow superbly mastered the way to drill through the auspices of ROTC in high school: "To the left flank, 'Arch! To the Rear, 'Arch!" The irony was that I loathed ROTC – the pompousness of the dim-witted Army instructors bent on cruelty, the absurd regimentation, the way boys whose fathers were part of the town's establishment got chosen to be Cadet Officers – soured me on the program. I could drill like a minstrel figure, but the powers that be read my feelings and chose me to carry the flag. It was their form of punishment. I chose not to. I claimed the pole that fit into the leather socket over my crotch was causing me excruciating pain. In fact it didn't bother me at all. But I wasn't going to be shamed into a flag carrying role. I resigned from ROTC and took gym, where three other drop outs and I shot hoops, the ball bouncing loudly in the cavernous, empty gym, the phys. ed. teacher away in his closeted office doing I know not what.

Now, scarcely six months later, I found myself in olive drab fatigues, top deck on the Marine Dragon, looking over the terrain as we docked in Yokahama for refueling and supplies before pushing on for Inchon, Korea. I looked down and there was an American sailor, strutting along, belonging to the area. Seeming to not have a care in the world. Barely a year before we had been at war with Japan, had dropped the atomic bomb on Hiroshima and Nagasaki, had been pouring out war films where enemy soldiers were called Japs and who wore little wire framed glasses and went about diabolically torturing prisoners until we got to bayonet them on some atoll. Scary little Nips! Now in the new reality I gazed beyond and there was Fujiama, snow-capped and impressive on the horizon. A picture of it was engraved on a tray back home. I had looked at that tray every day as I passed through the kitchen for years. Now the real thing rose in the distance. How many other things, after being seen countless times as an image in a movie or on a page, would show up in real life – the Eiffel Tower, Big Ben, the Brandenburg Gate? Every time it was as if I had been dropped into a movie. Here, looking off now at Fujiama. I was struck by its having seen the war come and go and it stood there unchanged.

Some of us on deck called down to the sailor below. He smiled and waved back. He had arrived. He was already there. He was the first Occupier I had seen. But not for long. I smelled Korea a few nautical miles before we landed. It was an overpowering scent that spread like a mist far and wide. I learned that its components were garlic and a sloshing over the top of honey carts that carried cargos of human shit along every road to be used as fertilizer on gardens by every thatched roof home. Once inhaled, it stayed with you forever like that of the old train station back home with its overflowing spittoons and sawdust mixed with creosol on the floors.

Before we deported there was one last chore we must undergo: a short-arm inspection. That was what it was called. A line snaked below deck back as far as the eye could see. Each soldier presented himself before a medic who sat in a chair and held a flashlight. A name and serial number was announced and someone closeby desk checked it off a list. Then the soldier pulled out his dick and presented it under the flashlight's glow. "Milk it down," the medic said to one after another in a bored voice. As I neared I hoped I wouldn't have too much trouble finding mine. Out it came as I rolled my eyes up and I milked it down. Nothing came out the tip. I did not have the clap. If they found someone on the ship with it I never learned. I don't think I'd have liked the medic's job although it would have been interesting, I guess.

Off the ship at last, a tightly packed duffel bag balanced precariously on my shoulder, fighting to keep my balance. Then on a train as darkness fell. The train was rusted and rickety and had no heat. We swayed and clattered onward. The hillsides we passed presented a galaxy of little pinpricks of light, strange but comforting somehow, showing that life of some sort was going on inside the thatched huts. Up and down the hillsides they shone, a ton of people inside, none showing outside. The ride was nothing like train travel back home where seats were covered in tight green material that showed the possibility of being cushioned but were not. On the ceiling pale yellow lamps glowed as you rocked along, news vendors and sandwich hawkers tiredly announcing their wares. No announcements, nothing on the troop train, except the steam that came from underneath. Finally our destination, the Repo Depot they called it. That was where we would get our assignments. I didn't know what to expect and that was for the better. The Army decided every thing for you. You didn't have to think. You got to worry but not to think.

We were put up in an old Japanese factory. Nearly everything from then on had the imprint of Korea's past occupiers, the Japanese, since they had occupied Korea periodically since 1592. Their most recent incursion was in 1910 and had only recently been thrown out in 1945. Here awaited us rows of bunks and a squawk box that let loose continually. The voice was dry and theatrical and the person never seen. "Keep your bunks orderly. No wrappers or butts on the floor. Orders will come in the morning for all men. You won't be forgotten. In the meantime, don't harass me and I won't harass you." Who the hell was this? Where the hell was he? The voice was transfixed with the word, harass. It appeared at the end of every speech. Had the person been given vocal training and orders himself? "Chow is at 0600. Where you'll be stationed will come shortly afterward. Don't harass me and I won't harass you."

I was assigned to an Engineering Battalion. I had trained at Knox for tanks, my head popped out of a Sherman turret, directing movement and firing. Somehow, without my asking, I'd been chosen to command. Maybe it was because I was tall and skinny and my head could reach high from the turret. I narrowly missed having it taken off by a tree limb as we rumbled on, ducking just in time. They, the ubiquitous "they", gave us the opportunity to fire a live shell at the end of a maneuver, thinking it was a treat, a reward. Actually it was. The whole tank shook and a shell exploded on target like the Fourth of July. I have to admit it was fun. I couldn't drive a car, but I was commanding a tank. Now I had my orders for the 42nd Engineering Battalion at a place called Yong Dong Po. I didn't know where that was or what it meant. It all seemed a dream. My buddies who had joined up with me in Tennessee were going elsewhere. Daffy Ducker kept his hands in his fatigue pockets, a cigarette dangling from his lips, a pose he'd often taken in our hometown. It passed for thinking. He wanted to appear tough and I guess he was, his mother giving the money he sent home to save to his father who was a drunk. He had a lot to be tough about.

Aberdeen was going to my outfit, Burden off somewhere else. I slung my duffle bag in a two-and-a half and the truck barreled down a dusty road that was pocked with holes as if hit by shells. Maybe it had been. We passed bicyclists with large loads on their shoulders. We passed women in white jackets on foot carrying loads on their shoulders taller than them. We careened around honey carts and civilian trucks that belched black smoke and couldn't do over 20. We seemed to hit every pocked hole on the way. The driver was black. Motor pools in Korea were run by blacks. Only blacks were in them. No one thought it unusual. That was just the way things were.

At Yong Dong Po I climbed out of the two-and-a-half with my duffle bag and claimed a bunk in a former factory building that reeked of motor oil and machinery. Bunks had been lined up for us as if in an infirmary. Night had fallen and most of us settled in for sleep. I couldn't. I had to brush my teeth although I debated for a few seconds whether I was required to or not. Back home my mother had instructed me to never go to bed without brushing my teeth. If you don't do so, they won't stay white any longer. Notice the heroes in movies. The good guys have white teeth. The bad ones don't. That simple. Boots untied, nothing buttoned up, I made it to the outdoor latrine, bumping by snoring, rustling comrades in their bunks. No one was in the latrine where a lone bare bulb hung. There were oil drums with wooden seats atop, a layer of lime at the bottom. A tin trough, yellowing and pungent, lay nearby. It was cold in the latrine. Only cold water ran from the tap. Shivering, I took out my toothbrush. I brushed my teeth.

* * *

In the morning our mess kits were loaded with blocks of powered eggs. I didn't drink coffee. I hadn't learned to yet. I got it down and from there things passed in a whirlwind, hardly giving me time to think. I felt rather than thought. I felt homesick and bereft, sad that the glories I had imagined, the gala of foreign romantic travels, had boiled down to a strange place that smelled of garlic and honey carts, to Korea. The Koreans weren't welcoming us with open arms. They came in all shapes, sizes, and ages but one thing they held in common: We were foreigners, taking over their land and they would get out of us what they could before they got us out. That's all they could do. We called them "gooks." Directives came down from on high not to do that, speeches made, editorials in Stars and Stripes, but we did it anyhow. It was too ingrained in us to call them anything else.

I am assigned to Company C in the 42nd Engineer Battalion and am milling about in our squad room one evening, wondering what was going on, when I hear someone cursing up a storm in a thick Southern accent. It goes on in a soft high voice, to the great appreciation of others, and then a small presence comes swaggering in. It is a Korean boy of perhaps nine years of age dressed in a cut-down Major's uniform, complete with bronze oak leaves on the epaulet of his officer's miniature tunic. Someone fashioned this uniform for him and he came swaggering in. "Kiss my ass and call me Charley you low bred dirty assholes." Everybody hooted. He even carried a swagger stick. It struck me that he must be the Company mascot, something like that, someone to affectionately keep around. He was someone called Major Lee. Every other person in Korea seemed to be called "Lee" or "Kim." But after his bravado parade in front of us I never saw him again or heard him mentioned. He became just another weird sight that came and went.

Another night, a short time later, I dropped by the Orderly Room where off to the side, in an adjoining room, a Korean man was down on the floor whimpering but not crying or speaking. Some other Koreans, in ROK military uniforms – on *our* side against Communists, I supposed – were beating the living shit out of him, asking and telling him things I couldn't understand. When they noticed me, they laughed, pointed at the man below – what a fun job we have! – nodding for approval. Strangely, the beaten man smiled at me, too. In their minds the man deserved a beating. I nodded back with a weak grin of my own. They beat him some more. The Korean garlicky smell rose in the air with each blow. I felt bad. I felt sorry for the man. I didn't know what to think of the ROK soldiers. We generally held them slightly above the general run of Koreans, but nothing more. At bottom, they were just another part of the strange scene. They were gooks.

In Tennessee I had owned a BB gun. Now I was handed my own personal M-1. I slept with it nearby. I could have shot up the whole company if I had wanted to. So could anyone else with one. But it never crossed my mind. I had learned the mechanism of the M-1 back in Basic Training. I could take the rifle apart in my sleep, and I was a surprisingly good marksman. I had learned well how to hold my breath and *squeeze* the trigger, never pulling back on it with a jerk. Soon I was carrying it on Guard Duty.

Guard Duty had never been mentioned at Fort Knox or, if it had, I had slept through the lecture. So much had been thrown at us in Basic Training that it was hard to keep things straight. Mostly what was learned in Basic was to be wary of Non Commissioned Officers, but do what they said no matter what, and to envy and be mystified by Officers and the way they lived. No one at Battalion Hdqs. in Korea brought up Guard Duty until one morning names were yelled out of those who would report for such at 1600 on the drill field. Among them: Bowers, RA14218267. "Be ready for full inspection then!"

I was ready, boots shined, rifle cleaned, but uncomfortable. What did you do on Guard Duty? It was something like Combat. No one explained it but you got the general idea of what it would be like. We had seen it done in movies. Everyone seemed to take it for granted that the answer was simple and no need for further explanation. Maybe it was so awful that no one wanted to think about it. On Guard Duty you would guard something. But what was it you guarded here in Korea and where? How would you go about it?

"*Present Arms*!" a creaky, high-pitched cry went out on the cracked concrete drill field that was about the size of the vacant lot beside our house in Tennessee where I used to play tackle football and get my bell run regularly. The Officer of the Day, a slack-jawed Second Lieutenant with pimples named Riggel, made a short speech. If anyone approached while we were on post we should call out, "Halt, who is there!" Later an Officer of the Day, a captain named Rothbart, would do an aria on how it should never be, "Who *goes* there!" That was for the movies, for the arty. The barrel-chested captain had a thing about "the arty." He did memorable arias every time he was Officer of the Day and was an enforcer of the rules. He went on and on about "hair." "I never want to see any Leopold Stokowskis around here. Never!" He was a little "arty" himself and had a beautiful speaking voice, like a radio announcer. I loved to hear him speak but was scared of him. The person told to halt should then identify himself. Then he must give the password. The password was something like "Scrambled eggs" or "Chestnuts." It changed with every tour. Lieutenant Riggel who had the pimpled faced passed by the row of us at "Present Arms." He didn't seem too sure of what he was supposed to do either. I looked straight ahead – I knew to do that – and now and then the Lieutenant took a rifle from someone's hands to give it a quick look. He didn't give himself time to really look it over. But it let us know that he was in charge. *Fall Out*!"

Carrying my M-1 and a clip of ammo, I hoisted myself up on a two-and-a-half along with ten others that had been chosen for Guard Duty, and we sat facing each other on benches in the back. The truck took off in a grinding roar and we weaved and bounced in the back for I knew not where. All I could think of was how pleasant it had been at this time back home, reading the afternoon paper, smelling the evening meal of fried chicken or beaten steak my mother was cooking and waiting appreciatively to dig in later under the shaded lamp that hung from the ceiling over our round oak kitchen table. In the truck, we rattled past thatched huts where outside men in dark vests and ballooning white pants gaped at us. Women in full white skirts frowned. What did they make of us? What could we make of them? Through the dust we stirred up came that smell of Korea I would never forget, of garlic and honey carts and centuries of wood burning fires. Koreans breathed it out, through their mouths and clothes and roads. I wanted to be back home. I was dropped off in the middle of nowhere along with one or two others. One was Meadow, who, like me, hardly needed to shave. He still had baby fat on his cheeks and a shy embarrassed half-grin on his face. We were guarding what looked like construction material that lay behind barbed wire. Darkness had fallen and a fire blazed in an oil drum. An oil drum was a necessary instrument here. We took dumps over one and now a fire blazed in another. Loose planks from somewhere fed the flames. The wind took the flames up high and black smoke mixed with sparks of fire curled around at the top. Faces were lit up starkly near it. I walked to my post a hundred yards or so away. Meadow was further along, around the corner of the barbed wire. I couldn't see him but knew he was there. He stands out faintly in my memory, a beardless boy, a little bit more lost than I was. I realized he had even less experience in life than me.

There was a chill in the air this night, a sharp notice that winter was on the way. I didn't believe I was restricted to one spot, standing still, so I moved around, stomping my feet. I looked around, scared but not exactly sure what of. Rumor had it that a soldier on another post had been ambushed recently and had his nuts cut off. That seemed pretty drastic and a horror. I had trouble seeing more than a few yards in front of me. Suddenly, I heard: "HALT! Who is there?"

"It's me," I said.

It was someone nearby. It was Meadow. I heard a shell locking into position, in a fumbling way, not cleanly. We had been told to load and lock when challenging anyone heard or seen approaching.

"For God's sake, don't point that gun at me. It's me!" I said. I figured he was one guy in the army I could tell what to do. It was pleasurable for once to be in that position and I didn't want to be shot by someone not knowing what he was doing. I didn't want to deal with Meadow with a loaded gun.

"You're not identifying yourself!" he called.

"I sat beside you in the truck!"

"It's not what we're supposed to do."

"O.K., I'll identify myself. But get that shell out of the chamber and quit pointing that gun at me. What are you? Crazy? You could kill someone. Your hands are shaking all over the place."

"O.K.," he said meekly.

I identified myself and gave the password.

Later, much later, it seemed hours, the two-and-a-half roared up and I climbed up and aboard. From then on, for a while, Guard Duty came about regularly and was a nightmare. Nothing was more dreaded. For a day or two before those for Guard Duty was posted my spirits began sinking. It stole into every thought. On Guard Duty you slept on cots in a special area. It was two hours Guard Duty and then four hours sleep. In the deepest sleep a rifle butt would strike the sole of your boot and the order came: "Get up. Get moving." If you went to sleep on post, or rather if you were caught, you could be sentenced to death. That was surely extreme and would never be carried out, but nothing could sound more dramatic. I did nod off a few times at first. I might be thinking about the girl I fantasized loving, but hadn't touched, back in Tennessee. It brought on a calm mellow romantic feeling. And then I awoke with a start to look around and see that no superior was anywhere near.

Then, as the weeks passed, it got cold. To be cold in Korea was not like being cold in Tennessee. In Tennessee I came home shivering from a walk downtown in winter and would warm myself over the register from the basement furnace below. Its soothing air went sensuously up my pant legs and the chill went away. Here, in Korea, when winter really set in, there was no escaping the numbing cold. Once before lights out I placed a glass of water beside my bunk and woke to find it frozen solid in the morning. We slept with our fatigues on, sometimes our boots, with whatever blankets we could find to pile on. I wrote home asking for blankets to be sent but my parents had trouble understanding the request. I was in the U.S. Army. Surely they had enough blankets. What kind of requests was that? Our Company never bathed through the winter. We cleaned ourselves the best we could from helmets filled with boiled water in the slapdash latrine. One buddy, as nice as could be, who never bitched or swore, who came from Ohio, got a nasty fungus infection that never went away. First one salve was tried, then another. Doctors came and went. The mean red streaks on his face that looked like athlete's foot would fade only to come back with a vengeance once he relaxed and thought it cured. It covered his face as he boarded the ship for trip home a year later.

It was not until spring that a shower became available in one of our many movements through the area. It was off the latrine where three or four nozzles spurted hot water over an enclosed plank floor. The news that π were at hand spread through the outfit. We couldn't talk about anything but that. We went in by shifts, officers and men together, all equal, and it was the first time I had all my clothes all off since we had landed in October. I still, many many years later, see the steam rising from naked bodies and feel the strong GI-issue soap in my hand going over my torso. I spot Lt. Phillips in the steam with that reddened bemused smile on his face. He had once been a West Point cadet and had been dismissed for some unclear reason which he never went into but had then gone on to a commission through the Regular Army and OCS. He revered the Army and West Point although West Point had thrown him out. He was as lyrical about it as General Douglas MacArthur. He was obviously a drunk and old for a lieutenant. He was loving the shower and singing to himself.

But before that miraculous spring day, many a mile had to be trod in Korea. Our squad in "C" Company lined up each morning after a meal of either a concoction of powdered eggs cooked solid or swimming in liquid. No fruit ever. Never milk. Coffee steamed. Most men smoked. I still hadn't recovered from a protected childhood and I never once, in Korea, indulged in either. I kept brushing my teeth every night or feeling guilty about it when I didn't. Our squad climbed aboard a two-and-a-half each morning, bouncing along on wooden seats, to some supposed construction or engineering site. It was then I was reminded that I was in the Engineers. But I could engineer nothing. Neither could anyone in our squad or maybe in Korea. We watched Koreans hoist lumber and bricks and do with them as they willed or what some plan somewhere dictated. I suspected that whatever we were doing was just the appearance of work, not work. Much later, in an entirely new persona, I worked for the State Department in Washington. I suspected the same there: Most of us were just shifting papers around, ears plugged into phones, appearing to work. Wherever real work was being done was done by others somewhere. We were "goldbricking" as the army put it back then. Against reason perhaps I never developed distaste for unions and their demands. Somewhere real work did get done and people must organize and get paid for it. That's how I felt and feel. If some didn't shoulder their load, so what? My tall taciturn gray haired father was a Union man. He was a telegrapher for the Southern Railway. Snow, sleet, tornado, he showed up. He never took a day off. He never called in sick. He actually never was "sick" as far as I could remember. In the 1930's Depression he was laid off and then put at temporary posts in the state away from home. War came and because of man shortage worked seven days a week, mostly through the night. He loved Roosevelt. He said, although no one had asked him, that Roosevelt liked the "little" man. My father was six foot two.

The two-and-a-half rumbled the pock-marked dirt road as we were taken to our posts, dropped off one by one, the

Corporal of Guard calling out our names. "Private Bowers!" I would hear, and I would swing down, my M-1, held by a strap from my shoulder. Fall was in the air. I remembered how innocently we had observed Halloween in Tennessee. We would throw leaves on someone's porch or write something on a neighbor's car window and then run like hell. I climbed to a tower, much like one used in concentration camps, from the war just finished. Up there, my M-1 parked beside me, I thought of the pool room back home and the click of balls and the muted sounds and the light that spread over the green felt of the table. Those thoughts were like a security blanket, protecting me from harm. I could see nothing over the rail of the tower except tarps pulled tight over equipment of some sort behind barbed wire. And then I heard a sound. I looked down and there was short, bandy-legged Captain Rothbart, Officer of the Day, looking up. He was wetting his lips and seemed to be waiting in sensuous anticipation. He had told us, in his professional radio announcer's voice, to have a shell locked into place when we challenged anyone. No excuses. You're in the army, men. You're not in the Boy Scouts. I came down the concentration camp ladder as fast as I could, trying to keep my balance, trying to put the clip in and sending a shell into the chamber, my helmet that was too large for me rolling around on my head. When I hit the ground there he was before me. I was still fumbling to get the shell in the chamber and a horrible, bone-chilling thought hit me. What if I shot him? What if my shaking hand hit the trigger and Captain Rothbart took one in the gut? I felt sorry for him already. I sensed that he was just playing the part of being a Captain as I was of being a Private. He didn't know any more about what he was doing than I did. "O.K., what's next?" he said, coaxingly. "Go on."

"Who is there?" I said.

"Officer of the Day," he crooned, in his syrupy voice, really enjoying it, "Captain Rothbart."

I guess he had forgotten about the password. I wasn't going to bring it up. My rifle was at port arms. He reached up, grabbed it, slid the bolt back and saw that a bullet was snug in the chamber. He handed it back. What more could we say? "Any disturbances tonight, soldier? Any activity?"

"Nothing I've seen, sir."

"Carry on." How he rolled those words out! It was melodic. I thanked the Lord I hadn't shot him. I climbed back up the ladder to the concentration camp tower, sat back down, thought about the girl I was in love with back in Tennessee but hadn't touched and mentally tried to push time forward for the two-and-a-half to return back in a roar and take me away.

Guard Duty knew no season. When the wide deep Han River froze solid in the dead of winter, solid enough to drive a truck over, when faces peered out of the fur-lined hoods of newly issued jackets, when two minutes outdoors and your eyebrows frosted, Guard Duty went on. My name went on the board, we had inspection and a few words from the Officer of the Day and then we roared off, cheeks numbed, fingers stiff inside gloves. I was dropped off near what I took to be a rice paddy. What now was I guarding? Like a faint breeze the thought often came to me that the Russians who loomed above the 38th parallel might decide to descend in a massive lightning like stroke. I would be of no use to stop them. I came to that conclusion and I could already see myself going to pieces because, of what I had seen of the army, we weren't that much good at anything. But I would stand my post, by God, come what may, like my father had stood his post, pecking out the Morse code at the railroad depot, come what may. I was no coward. I was just imaginative.

That night I heard no sound, I saw nothing move in the environs. Everything, including me, was freezing. After awhile I could think of nothing else. I tried to shift my weight. I tried to stomp and move about. I tried in vain. And, although, I could not lift my jacket sleeve back and see the time, I realized that the truck was overdue in picking me up. No sound anywhere except the wind that whistled by. I strained to hear the comforting sound of the two-and-a-half somewhere, strained to picture a buddy behind the wheel pulling up jovially and letting my relief swing down and take my place. After awhile I could barely move my head to see down the lonesome deserted road from where a truck might come. I waited and waited, two hours after my relief was due to arrive when suddenly, out of nowhere, one appeared. I could have cried if tears could have flowed. I tried but couldn't move. "Get him up, men!" someone yelled.

Hands were at my elbows and under my knees and I was hoisted up into the truck. "You're late," I was able to say. "Where the hell you been?"

"Everything's frozen. You're lucky we got this one going."

Six months before I had been playing basketball in an overly heated gym on my high school team. We usually lost. I thought of that.

* * *

Before the weather got nasty, a short time after landing in Korea, when I was first getting a feel for the place, I got a pass from the Orderly Room to go into Seoul. I simply asked for one and got it. I tried to get a buddy or two to go with me but none would. They would rather stay in barracks and vegetate. I wanted adventure. Seoul was the Capitol. I had to check it out. But how to get there? I had my pass but no info on how to get to the capitol and then back to Yong Dong Po. Checking around I found some two-and-a-half's idling near our outfit's gate. The driver of one said he headed for Seoul. Did I want a lift? Twilight shadows fell over the truck. Some GI's were already aboard, gloomily looking at their feet. Trucks were rattling in and out of the gate, an MP checking them through. "Do you take us back later?" I said.

"Trucks go back and forth all the time. Just grab one."

"Just grab one?"

"Yeah." He had the superior tone of a veteran, someone who knew everything you needed to know about any and everything. Having more service time than someone who'd just arrived gave you that attitude. I later came by this well-earned attitude myself. He drummed his fingers on the steering wheel. "Well?"

"What's in Seoul?"

"A USO with some broads from the States. Lots of troops and gooks. Some Russians. They're weird, man."

"And just grab any truck back that's going my way?"

"Yeah. Just make sure they're going by the 42nd Engineering Battalion. That's all."

It came to me that there might be a problem. Any truck might not include one going by the 42nd. But the motor ran and other GI's were aboard. I was in my sun-tans and cap and the weather was warm then. I had a pass. I just had to be back for reveille, and I had always been up for the extravagant. Hadn't I joined the army and fought to get overseas? In Tennessee where opportunities weren't abundant I had ventured into surrounding towns at the first opportunity, by bike or railroad pass or hitching a ride. I remember Erwin, Tennessee, 15 miles away. When I was 16 I had hitched a ride there in the summer to see what it was like, asking no one's permission. I couldn't get over it. They had their own newspaper, their own drugstore to hang out in. There were girls, looking like the girls from my hometown but they had different homes and home rooms in school, different teachers. There were movie theaters, a YMCA, and

I knew no one on the street. It proved that there was life elsewhere, something like finding life on Mars. I had no trouble getting back to my hometown. I just put out my thumb and caught a ride. It was easy back then.

I swung in the truck and squeezed between two GI's who hadn't anything to say. The two-and-a-half careened out the gate of the 42nd Engineering Battalion and we were off for Seoul.

The truck left whirls of dust in the air behind it. The countryside was the same as always, on the road to Seoul: Thatched huts, old men in ballooning white pants and thoughtful expressions, women in long white skirts behind them avoiding any eye contact. We passed rice paddies, vendors who squatted behind an array of cigarettes and trinkets, to sell to what buyers I couldn't imagine. We hit craters big enough for the moon, we swayed, the motor ground away as gears grindingly changed. We got past the Han River and not long after we were on streets that accommodated rickety civilian trucks and ancient street cars with prongs socked into wires above. Passengers inside were impossibly jammed together, leaning out windows, one body on top of another, none complaining. It was the way things were. There was a train station with mobs milling about. Korean blared forth from loud speakers. The truck came to a jerky stop. We were in front of a building that held a large sign that said, USO, Troops Welcome. Soldiers jumped down from the truck. I followed. Our truck then barreled away, the driver presenting a brief wave of so long. I saw that there was a line of two-and-a-half's nearby, motors running, getting set to go somewhere. Surely I could get a ride back to Yong Dong Po and the 42nd. Or I told myself so.

I didn't see any familiar face in the USO, no one from my outfit. I ate a dough nut but didn't drink the coffee, the only provided fare. I watched a ping pong game and felt I could beat anyone there but no one asked me to join in. The players apparently were from the same outfit, different from mine, and didn't know how to handle outsiders. Here I was in the midst of GI's who were strangers. The few USO hostesses were surrounded and taken and if they hadn't been I wouldn't have known what to do. I hadn't joined the army and crossed an ocean for this. I wanted to see the sights. I wanted to see Korea. I wanted to see what Seoul was like. I left.

I made a bravado move into a narrow street or two, all bustling with Koreans, and then hustled back to the line of trucks, making sure they were still there. I walked near the giant railway station but feared going inside and getting engulfed and not able to get out, pushed on a train by the mob. After a few streets and inhaling various bouquets of strangeness, I decided to call it quits and get back to the safety of my outfit. I knew my way around there. I needed a familiar face. I stood and looked up at a driver whose truck rumbled in the line. "Going near the 42nd?" I yelled.

"The 42nd what?"

"The 42nd Engineering Battalion."

"Never heard of it."

"Who might?"

"Keep trying!"

I did, up and down the line. Some knew of it, some knew of Yong Dong Po, but none were going that way. The USO was closing. Lights were dimming inside and soldiers were walking out but none going in. I was 11-years-old again, on Main Street back home and the town's 9:30 curfew was about to sound from a plant's steam whistle and everyone under 16 found wandering around downtown was taken to the jailhouse and their parents called to pick them up. Or, I imagined over and over, they weren't called; I languished in jail. The dreaded curfew had been abolished after a brief terrifying run but the memory would live in my mind forever: To be alone at night, no one to help, no way to get back home, a policeman coming to nab you. What would they think back at the base if I couldn't get back? Here's Bowers' empty bunk and he has missed reveille. What kind of soldier is he? Give him a pass and he disappears. Court marshal him, throw him in the stockade. Who are we letting in the army these days anyhow? Would I just wander the streets of Seoul forever or be cut up and thrown in the Han River? Would anyone come to find me? What?

It may have been the fourth or fifth truck I came to, but it seemed forever and I thought it even a fluke or mistake when a cheery-faced driver called down, "Yeah, the 42nd. I can swing by there. Jump in."

"It'll be no trouble? You can do it? You can?"

"Take it easy, soldier. I'll get you there. Get in."

I got in, I got back to my outfit, relief loosening the flesh from my bones. We bounced along, and in short order I forgot about my near panic that I might be stranded in a strange foreign city and never heard from again. Back safely in the squad room I talked about the sights I had seen to those who hadn't seen Seoul, embellishing a little. I had another year to get through in this far-off place and I was already thinking about how the return ship might roll and pitch on the high seas.

* * *

How I dreamed of an apple, just a plain tart apple I could bite into, and a glass of milk. I thought of girls. Ernie Banks, a boy I had gone to school with, from first grade through high school, sent me pictures, ripped from Life magazine, of girls with good legs in shorts and busty girls in tight sweaters. I don't know why he did it except for the fact that from an early age ruminations over sex had been the glue that kept our friendship together. He didn't play sports. The pictures of these girls – in the magazine's spread on the current crop of co-eds or some such – came like miniature care packages, accompanied by scrawled comments from Ernie on lined paper: "This one looks like Nancy Jane Helton, giggling cause she's wanting it. Come back and get some of that stuff. How's the army?"

I wrote home to my parents. They had never been out of the country and only as far west as Oklahoma City where they had gone on their honeymoon. The stationery was army issue light blue and tissue thin. I wallowed in how much I appreciated the old days, trying to live them again by describing them – the rituals of our home life: My mother and aunt visiting Mrs. Weems across the street of an evening; my father walking silently off to the depot where he worked as a telegrapher; Mr. Winters delivering milk on the front porch at dawn. It was as if I was calling back a hallowed time and place that had somehow died. It was embarrassing but I couldn't help it.

I wrote to the girl I hadn't kissed and that was embarrassing, too. She hadn't asked for me to write her. She undoubtedly thought it strange and maybe a little crazy that she was now getting letters on tissue blue paper telling about odd ball characters who were in my outfit and what I had eaten for breakfast. She always wrote back politely and girlishly as if we were in some ritual that neither of us understood but which she must honor. I was sure Daffy Ducker was writing to her, too. I wondered what he wrote. His outfit was down in Pusan.

So little did any of us understand, we of tender years, most of us still teenagers – Jews from Brooklyn, Pollocks from Chicago, rednecks from the South, a potpourri of representatives concentrated into the 42nd Engineering Battalion of the 24th Corps. We had been jerked suddenly from our secluded, particular homes and thrown into a culture that had been turning out *kimchee* and producing calligraphy long before Custer was wiped out by the Red Man at Little Big Horn. Maybe before Christ they had a civilization going. We were here as Occupiers, the Boss. Our history was filled with mistakes, some real lulus if we had only studied and thought about it.

And now here I was, heading once again in Seoul in the back of a bouncing, rocking two-and-a-half, on leave for the evening, getting more confident each trip I took. I didn't have enough hair to comb, compliments of the Korean barber, and was decked out in sharply pressed Sun Tans, compliments of an iron somewhere in a thatched hut off base where laundry was done for a carton of cigarettes, ready for adventure and to push the boundaries of human experience. This meant finding Bung Chung Street where the clubs and dance parlors were. The intelligence about the dance halls was supplied by Private Aberdeen who immediately knew everything there was to know after once landing in Korea. "Yeah, man, there's girls galore down in them Bung Chung dives. You won't believe it. Bring along some occupation funny money and see what it'll bring. Or a carton of cigarettes."

It was mandatory to seek these clubs out and find out the score, as mysterious an urge as the one to discharge the juices that had suddenly shown up at puberty from a few years back. The army, military service, chooses, for them the right age for you to prepare to fight and to send you, as it was now doing with me to a far off land – but it must not be forgotten that it's also the age when your juices are running rampant. Plus the frontal lobe, as I learned later, had not developed fully and you were not so aware of consequences and dangers as you would at 40. Just the sight of Bung Chung Street, bursting at the seams with dim shops, jangled music over raspy loud speakers, and dance hall marquees featuring names like "Dancing Girls" was enough to set the blood racing and the knees weaken. Here at last were females who were dangerous and exciting and beckoned like Circes from the shore. Some clubs had stark military notices that said, "OFF," which wasn't strictly paid attention to. GI's still trickled in, looking over their shoulders, on the outlook for MP's. If these GI's were going in and not nabbed, why not me? The ones deemed "OFF LIMITS" probably had the real stuff, the others too tame and for the weak. The "OFF LIMITS" ones stood out.

It is early evening in good weather, the clubs lit up, music blaring, and I find myself in a wedge stealthily easing into a forbidden one. There are more people inside than one might expect. I spot a couple of Russian soldiers in their trademark grayish tunics and black boots sitting morosely at a table. Never had I seen more than one or two together. We never knew how many were stationed in Seoul. And what they were doing there in the first place wasn't brought up. Immediately after the War things were pretty chaotic, far and wide. The Russians, what there were of them, were far from home as we were. Never did I see one in Seoul that seemed happy, that even smiled. They glowered. The prospect of something resembling sex had drawn them here as it had us. We didn't communicate. What was there to say?

I purchased some dance tickets with our funny money, our occupation bills of exchange. A dollar or two allowed me to spend some time with one of the girls (but not to dance in this dance hall). And not to do anything else, at least not there. And girls there were. They all smiled, one and all. On the street no woman smiled nor was there ever a greeting or eyes that met and lingered. It was revolutionary now to see all these smiles coming at you all at once with come hither looks. No transition whatsoever to put them – poor things, I think now – in the carnal lineup of the mind. Even a dead woman could get in there, though, if you weren't careful in that long ago day. Their cheeks rouged, their lips a scarlet swath, their cleavages plunging. At least those who first got my attention. Others were prim in the traditional white Korean jackets and long black skirts. We'd only been occupying Korea for a little over a year, and look at what had happened! A dancehall. Women with rouged cheeks and flaming red mouths. Tickets!

Most were too short or too anxious or too shy or too something or other although I was not constitutionally able to turn anyone down with my funny money. Suddenly one who stood on a bandstand where no band played caught my eye and wouldn't let loose. I wasn't used to that. No one in high school ever did that. The girl I was in love with and never had kissed ducked her head often when I looked her way. I was devoid of experience, 100 percent. I knew how to fire an M-1 on target but not how to kiss or do anything much else with a girl. She smiled, as if we had always known each other. I came over and spoke to her, up there on the bandstand. "I'm Miss Kim," she said, still smiling, "how much time you want spend with me?"

"How about till the dawn's early light?" I said. Cavalier as hell. How in the world was I able to come up with that? I felt cocky.

"Give me tickets."

I handed over a handful. She had that smile. She was interested in me. By God, she was interested in me. I wasn't used to that. "You big strong American soldier."

I weighed 140 pounds at six-foot-two and could hardly lift myself into a two-and- a-half without help. "You sweet little Korean girl," I said. I had to say something.

"You want meet outside? It difficult, but I like you."

"When?"

"I don't know. You get more tickets."

I purchased more tickets. I realized I actually stood a chance of going off for the night with young Korean girl named Miss Kim. I had no idea what would happen. I would be in her care. She wore an American-styled skirt and platform shoes. She would meet me outside. I would go with her to wherever. I was not afraid any more in Seoul, Korea, because I knew where the USO was with its bevy of two-and-a-halfs out front, motors growling, one of which was surely going to or past my outfit no matter when I showed up. The awesomeness of the potential made me weak. "Outside," Miss Kim said. "Look for me, But no look *at* me. Follow only."

I thought I understood. Could it be, could it be? I waited outside on Bung Chung Street by the side entrance. GI's passed all around me. Dust rose and strange loud music crackled from somewhere. MP's in Jeeps, on the outlook for something, passed. I waited and waited and then she slipped out that side door, a brief glance my way and then she took off down a side street. I followed behind, not too close, not too far back. We passed shops that all looked alike, people hunched over bowls of food. There was a small park, there were old men smoking from long pipes, and then there were no GI's in sight, no MP's on patrol. She kept determinately walking and I kept determinately following. At last she paused before a house that looked like all the other houses, glanced over her shoulder, the first time she had done so since we started, put her finger to her lips and entered, leaving the door cracked open for me to follow. Inside she whispered as I bent far over to hear, "Make no sound. Father and brothers kill if they hear."

I half believed her, but didn't want to test it. Shoes off and in my hand as she motioned for me to do I tiptoed behind as she led me down a hallway to a room that held not one stick of furniture. I took it that this was how Koreans lived – no furniture and with heated floors and no open fires inside. No beds but rolled cloth cylinders for head rests or pillows. No pictures on the walls. It was the first Korean home I'd been in. Miss Kim sat with her knees drawn up, hugging her legs. She leveled a look at me without the usual smile. We were nearing a decision of some sort, but, no matter what, I was thoroughly proud of myself. I had talked a woman who liked me into spending the night with me. It was a first. If we spent the night together, maybe something would happen. But what?

I went to embrace her to get the ball rolling, to see what would happen, but she wagged her finger in my face. "No noise. Brothers kill you if they hear."

I heard faint noises from an adjacent room – what sounded like glasses clinking and guttural words exchanged. There was a rustle of clothes. I pictured a scene, suspected a lot, but accepted what she said. This was her home, where she lived, she was part of a family. That's what my instinct told me. But all I had to go on, the memory I was left with, was hardly more than the muffled sounds on the other side of a thin wall. It was just Miss Kim and me. Bored, or pretending to be bored, she asked for, and got, a few bills of funny money from my wallet. She had stopped smiling or showing any signs of endearment and now had begun frowning. It was not clear what she had done, or what I might expect her to do, for this handover of cash. I sure didn't know. It was as if she had mastered part of a ritual but not all of it. What next?

We spent the night together like Puritans in New England on a cold winter's night. Chastely. I lay with my head on a hard cylinder while Kim kept going outside, to other rooms, to do I knew not what, and then softly returning. She seemed to be catching bites to eat but she didn't offer me anything. I wouldn't have eaten it anyhow because of strict warnings about Korean food. I caught a heavy scent of garlic from her every time she returned. When I tried to talk she put her finger over her lips. I lost interest in talking anyhow, and finally a pale light started creeping in. Dawn. I didn't have the energy for another try at an embrace.

As I stood on the dirt road outside, having nodded up and down in farewell, as she kept putting the finger to her lips for silence, I wondered if I had done anything wrong.

Had my one feeble lurch at her been too aggressive and gauche? What was actually going on? Had she not known what to do as well as me? Was she as new to all this as much as me? In the morning light, her lipstick gone, she looked no older than me. And were her brothers (or someone) in the next room, ready to slit my throat? I didn't want to find out.

All I knew was that I was in the middle of nowhere in a foreign land and it was daybreak and I had been in high school only six months before. I thought of the girl I was in love with back there but had never kissed. I then thought of the girl I'd just spent the night with but had never touched or kissed when I heard a truck's grinding roar come to a halt in a whirl of dust. A black face under green fatigue cap leaned out the window. "Where you going, man?"

"Hey. The 42nd Engineering Battalion."

"Never heard of it."

"Thanks anyhow."

I wasn't worried. With some army service under my belt, in and out of Seoul a few times, I had no fear I wouldn't find a lift. Actually, miraculously, I found the USO and its line up of trucks out front, all roaring to go. None were going my way. Then I remembered that my pass to go into Seoul was not for unlimited time. I had better get back to my outfit. I drifted down to the highway, if a wider than average crater-pocked road could be called such, where trucks were barreling in that direction. I tried to flag one down but it didn't stop although the driver saw me waving. I slumped onward, perked up by the thought that I had spent the night with a girl in her home, if that was her home. A two-and-a-half stopped beside me and I hadn't waved. Two black soldiers rode in the cab. The one by the window spoke: "Where you going?"

"The 42nd Engineers. Know of it?"

"No. But yell if we get near. Jump in if you want."

That was good enough for me. I climbed in and found a horde of black faces. I accepted that fact, like a new born baby accepts everything in the new world he finds himself in. Never would have happened in Tennessee, never would a truckload of blacks stopped to give me a lift. But this was Korea in 1946 before Truman had desegregated the troops. Back then, when I was in service, blacks had their own outfits and mostly ran motor pools for some reason. It was like a regiment of chauffeurs scattered over the countryside.

We rumbled away and I kept my eye peeled for familiar territory that announced my outfit, ready to yell, "Stop!" Or rather, "This is it. May I get off here?" I wanted to be polite, constrained by the leftover feelings from Tennessee. Like more than one Southerner who'd grown up under Jim Crow I felt uncomfortable with segregation but it was so pervasion, touching so many subtle and overt parts of the social contract that I didn't know what to do. I just knew it was wrong. I could tell, in that truck ride back then, that they didn't know what to do with me either, a white boy with a twang. They were nice to me. They were giving me a lift, not the other way around. Then I sensed, as they began to joke among themselves, that they had forgotten about me or didn't care that I was among them, and we were thousands and thousands miles from home.

A tall rather jumpy soldier – a smoked version of Aberdeen – cackled and wisecracked and couldn't sit still. He joked about the women who plodded along the side of the road, most carrying gigantic loads on their shoulders. They didn't know what he was yelling about and wouldn't look at him. I didn't either. A sergeant with a mournful face looked disgusted with the soldier. But others laughed and joined in. The soldier held a rock in his hand, from a cache he carried in his side fatigue pocket. He jiggled it, looking over the side, standing and swaying. "Dumb ass fucking country, how come you got my sorry ass sent over here?" he said. "Look at that gook!"

It was one of those old men with a wispy beard and a stovepipe hat. You saw them along every road, on every street, in every shop. "Who wants to bet I can't knock that hat off?

No one had time to answer. The rock whizzed off and missed. Another one left as the old man stood in bafflement, gazing at us, not moving, frozen in time. It missed, too, but not by as much. A strong side of me wanted to show my solidarity with these soldiers, to go along with the laughter. But I knew it was wrong but didn't know what to do about it. When I was dropped off at my outfit I thanked one and all but felt shame. The incident left an indelible impression. Years later, when we were first sending troops to another Asian country and calling them advisors I knew, without anyone telling me, it was wrong.

Back at base I wrote voluminous V-mail letters, they were called, on the tissue blue stationary. I wrote my old childhood friend, Ernie Banks, and could count on a reply, always with the same refrain, what most 18-year-old boys had on the minds. ("Nancy Jane Fitzgerald wants news about you. You should get some of that stuff when you get back. I saw some hairs getting outside her bathing suit last summer.") I heard from my former cadre sergeant from basic training at Fort Knox, who had wanted me to become cadre myself at Knox and not go to Korea. He was serving out his enlistment, a World War II vet, not charmed by the military. He liked me for some reason. ("Same old bullshit here," he wrote. "Can't wait to get out of this son of a bitch.") I wrote my parents, rhapsodizing on the joys of home and how I wanted to return. ("Boy, when I get back I'll go to the movies with you, Dad. I can't wait for that fried chicken you cook on Sundays, Mom. Boy oh boy, I'll walk to town. I'll read Charles Dickens.") They were embarrassing and later in life

I burned them because I thought they impinged on a sophistication and cynicism I was honing.

The 42nd was constantly moving; we had abandoned the damp, concrete floored factory building from Japanese occupation days and for a time quartered ourselves in a long narrow Quonset hut with a stove in the middle. Everything seemed temporary, our quarters, our food, our lives at times. There was never a fresh egg, but an avalanche of chicken. Somehow chicken overflowed from Australia. Maybe they had too many chickens or orders got fouled up. For hot food we had creamed chicken in one form or another, cooked in every form imaginable but never fried chicken nor roasted chicken or in any form recognizable from what we had in the States. I grew sick of it, we all grew sick of it. It didn't taste like chicken. The eggs weren't eggs, they were powdered eggs. It was a holiday to get s.o.s., shit on a shingle, from tinned beef. Never were religious dietary laws met. No fish on Friday, never any other day of the week for that matter. Pork might have slipped in in some form or another but never as bacon or chops. Back to dreaming about a tart hard apple and peanut butter on soft white bread, washed down with fresh milk.

So much was play acting about what was "normal" back in the States, things to remind us of normality when we were positioned an axe handle away from maniacs from the North who might suddenly descend on us. Every time the lights dimmed or went out, more than one of us thought, *"They're coming!"* What would I do? Would I go to pieces if shells flashed by and soldiers in gray tunics came forward like banshees? Could I raise my M-1? No, I pictured myself wishing I was back in Tennessee while immobile as if electrocuted, shaking and barely moving, unable to act. What had I got myself into? Of course our top generals told us how we were guardians of democracy, here to protect freedom, whatever that was. Had I signed up for that in Tennessee? I was Regular Army. I had signed up, I had volunteered. K.V. Kaltenborn, a political sage of the airways back home, paid a visit and told us what fine soldiers we were, what a fine job we were doing, how brave we were. No one knew what he was talking about.

It was announced that in Seoul there was a university. Soldiers could sign up for classes – in what it wasn't clear. In English, I trusted. I made a half-hearted attempt or two to find it among the broken roads, jammed streets, and dust in the air. It was in there somewhere among quite imposing, white marble government buildings that hadn't been damaged or totally neglected. I never found it nor figured out how I could attend if I still pulled duty with my outfit that was moving around over the countryside. It was unclear, but was an another example of how the powers that be wanted to give the impression to us, and possibly to themselves, that "normalcy" was there somewhere – like real hot food that came solely, and over and over, from frozen chicken from Australia. It gave me the chance to write home, saying I was looking forward to attending college while in the army, in Korea.

Nor was I against the illusion of normalcy or trying to make life a little better in this glorified foxhole that moved around. In late autumn of 1946 we moved to a compound that included an antiquated gym. We slung our duffle bags into four-and-a-half ton trucks that stood there roaring and the next thing found ourselves in new quarters. No one explained anything. The cry had come, "Pack your gear, men, we're moving out!" and that was it. A year before it had been the Japanese in their crazy caps with ear flaps; now there were basketball hoops along with four balls and expectation that some fun could be had. It needed though someone in Special Services (not to be confused with the gung-ho Special Forces that came along later to wreck havoc) someone to hand out balls and make sure they were returned, someone to think up events and stage entertainment. It was obvious. Through the chaos I proposed myself. We were getting a new First Sergeant, the old one happily reassigned back to the States. He had been a smooth-talking operator who got things done in a low key manner. Now, with no one getting down to the nitty gritty, much was left to those who could think up ordinary things like when was lights out (and extraordinary things, like my assigning myself to Special Services and no one objecting and no paperwork necessary.) The officers were too busy preening and waiting for cocktail hour. We thought up things more as if we were in the huddle in sandlot football than in "going by the book," whatever book that might be and whatever regulations might be in it. No one in the Orderly Room or elsewhere contradicted me when I said I would move into one of the rooms above the gym, hand out the balls, and think up entertainment. No one seemed to notice that I wouldn't then have to fall out at reveille then and go out on the line and supervise Koreans doing road work or something or other as others had to do. We were in Korea, had just begun the occupation after the Second World War. Some of us were thinking of what our roles might be on this foreign soil, how to operate, just as those who had sent us over were doing back in Washington. We were muddling through.

I was writing home. I was thinking of home where images of peanut butter sandwiches, cold milk, and an apple had once been at the ready. Could read the paper back there and look at the funnies. It was Saturday afternoon and I went to the pool room where I had a hot dog on a soft bun with pickle sauce, mustard, and chopped onions. The girl behind the counter was blonde and thin with the outline of breasts beneath her jacket. She had the beginnings of a smile. I shot nine ball under a hanging fluorescent lamp that shone over the table. Nothing was hurried ever. Chalk powder and cigarette smoke filled the air. I saw my buddies every day.

One I saw especially, my main buddy, was Daffy Duck, now stationed down in Pusan.

I inherited through the auspices of Special Services, or from somewhere, a record player and one record. It was miraculously there just as the basketballs and nets had been waiting in the gym below. The lone record was piano music from Art Tatum. I had never heard of him, but, boy, how he could ripple the ivories. It was so unlike music I was used to in Tennessee just as most of the troops I ran across were different from anything I knew existed on earth. I plugged the battered phonograph in, fit the 78 rpm on the turntable, and played Art Tatum over and over and over. Many years later I heard music coming from a jukebox in a Greenwich Village. It was so pleasing, so different from the other selections. It was the taste of a Madeline. It was Tatum whom I hadn't heard in over 30 years, but it all came back.

A Texan moved into the room over the gym in Korea. I think of him as someone called Jack. He had black hair, an athletic build, and he seldom smiled. We should have got along fine, but something impeded it. He said, and it was undoubtedly true, that he had played football in high school and he gave off the impression that he had a solid family background. All of which should have made him a prime candidate to be a buddy. Not so. It may have been that his solid, unsullied background kept his mouth shut when bawdy barracks talk began and outlandish bravado broke out. There was a whiff of primness about him, Jack from Texas. The army had a saying for nearly every psychological moment in life. For Jack, from Texas, it was: "He wouldn't say shit if his mouth was full of it." I figured his background was not dissimilar from mine, though. Maybe that was what burned me up. Why didn't he try to break free and see what the world had to offer? He was a Methodist. He was kept under wraps by something. I wanted to lie beside a Korean girl. I wanted to get drunk, see what it was like, and then be able to talk about it. I wanted adventure. I wanted to wear a uniform home with a ribbon or two on my chest. Playing basketball against Jack in the gym I could easily lock him down so he couldn't shoot. I could dribble past him, feint left and then right, and then unload into the basket. He could do nothing against me. That was another thing. He should have been tougher. What was the point of coming from Texas if you weren't tough?

Before long the room became not so much private quarters for Special Services (me) but more a place where any loose stone that wanted a berth and could work around the Orderly Room, the system, and the absence of a First Sergeant to forbid it, could throw his duffle bag down and move in. Later I lived in a fraternity house where members came and went to take up spare bunks and answer to no one. No rules were enforced. No pictures were on the wall. It was far from civilization. It reminded me of life in the room over the gym in Korea.

A few of us thought up trips to Seoul and to the countryside. Once we commandeered a truck from the Motor Pool, I forget with what excuse, grabbed our rifles and took off to practice marksmanship. Someone just suggested it, like a college prank, and those of us who were antsy and needed release climbed aboard. No one needed to go out on line duty that day, a Sunday, and Jack from Texas lay in his bunk writing letter after letter home. We bounced over a dusty, crater-pocked road to end up near a stream out in the middle of nowhere. There were lots of middles of nowhere in Korea then. A clip went in, a shell into a chamber, and we took turns, aiming at an empty C-ration tin placed on a rock, then pulling the trigger. You felt giddy, sighting down the rifle, no one supervising you, free to just bang away. The reports echoed in the hills. No one came running, no one told us to stop. They would have been crazy to do so anyhow.

Down stream a half dozen women in their traditional white jackets and full black skirts watched with frowns on their faces. They made no move to scurry off. They didn't look worried; they didn't look alarmed as we fired away. They just impassively watched from perhaps twenty feet away, squatting, and beating laundry against rocks. They would beat a piece of cloth against a rock a few times and then look up. They weren't looking for approval as the men did when they beat someone up for whatever reason. Women had probably been doing laundry in the stream this way since before Christ was born. I'd been holding a rifle, off and on, for about six months.

That was all it was that day, a day etched in my memory that lasts vividly until this day, women by a stream, beating laundry against large rocks while we fire round after round at tin cans not many feet away. They didn't greet us with open looks and neither did we them.

Not long after this fresh-air jaunt into the countryside it got cold. Christmas loomed and I got presents from home: Canned goods that I had asked for and my parents couldn't understand why. It was as if I was in a prisoner of war camp but the war was over. I also got a Boliva watch and an identification bracelet that simply spelled out my name. I wore it proudly even though I slept with dog tags on, like everyone else. I handed out slices of salami and pieces of squished Whitman chocolates to those who caught me about to take a sample or taking one. But I guarded practically everything else like Silas Marner. Christmas was coming, snow was falling, and this was the first time I had been away from home during this holiday season. I wanted to save the goods until later and keep some presents unopened or at least not eaten in the spirit of the Yuletide. I was proud that I had folks who would and could send me such bounty, but guilty that others may not have gotten a windfall or more likely anything at all. I didn't like the look when someone got a glimpse of the treasure and then eyed me. And who knew who might be in wandering in the room at any given time? A new resident in the room was Kelso, a likeable fat-cheeked malcontent who had something to do with mess supplies and the kitchen and who had talked his way out of staying in the regular barracks and into our room over the gym because he kept odd hours. Deep into mornings he lay in the folds of a ton of blankets, a half-cocked smile on his plump face, dreaming away while our comrades from the barracks rode off in the deadly chill for line duty. I felt a tinge of guilt for living a free lance life in the room myself but I was sure Kelso had no qualms. No matter though, he found something to bitch about, making it almost an art form that was in itself entertaining.

"Fuckin' gook coming around in the morning causing all that commotion. Don't he know some of us need our sleep?" That reminded him of why the Korean came around in the morning in the first place. "Cold as a well digger's asshole here. Why can't the son of a bitch at least come by earlier? Cold enough to freeze the balls off a monkey. What the fuck we paying him for anyhow!"

The "gook" was a Korean, as chubby as Kelso, nicknamed Half-Bright, a permanent good-natured smile plastered on his face, seeking to please. He was in charge of getting the wood stove going in the morning so that we Americans, us foreigners, could wake to its warm glow. He gathered any spare wood he found scattered about, from discarded crates to abandoned buildings that had fallen or building projects that were going up. Sometimes, I suspected from buildings that were standing and in good use. He picked up any loose board that wasn't nailed down. He brought them in, cradled in his arms, and started a fire by dousing it first with a splash of kerosene. He might be inventive in finding wood but he was lazy in getting a fire started, for the wood was often damp or green. Whatever he did he did with a smile and he got tips for his trouble. We threw tips around – to those who washed and ironed our laundry, those who got film developed, those who did anything that saved us from doing it. We could have been colonials in the time of the Raj and Gunga Din. He appeared in a Japanese military cap with ear flaps that hung down loosely. He was more than comfortable in the system: Get an early morning fire going, do any little odd job that came along, get a tip.

The system must have figured out that some of us had too good a deal, too: Being excused from reveille and guard duty and more or less going our own way. Things changed though when the new Top Kick arrived. He was a sharp-eyed man with unhappiness written all over his face, someone who was going to make us as unhappy as he was. He'd received a battlefield commission in World War II, had re-uped to serve out his time for retirement and been reduced in grade to non-commissioned officer status to do so. Not long before he had worn a captain's silver bars, had been served in the officers' mess, been saluted, and now he took orders from 19 and 20-year-olds who'd been through OCS. But he was going to hang on and get that pension. This was Sergeant William Weldon from Texas and he sent out an announcement that everyone must stand reveille, no excuses. That included those sorry asses in the little room above the big gym who'd been getting away with setting their own hours.

It was a cold morning, that day, no colder than usual, but the sky was turning a sharper blue than usual, cloudless. First light was breaking. Those of us in the little room cursed and hacked up phlegm and began pulling on boots. That is, all of us except Kelso. He lay curled up, his head buried in the blankets. "Kelso, up and at 'em!" some one yelled. "The new Top Kick is down there. You're going to get on the shit list for sure."

"Fuck off," he said, his usual reply to any request or order. Somehow he got away with it because he supposedly knew how to stop the Australian chickens from coming to the mess hall, which never did stop coming after he came aboard.

That day, that bone chilling day, the rest of us from the battalion stood on rubble that passed for a parade ground and faced our new Top Kick, Sergeant Weldon. He looked spiffy in shined boots and clean field jacket. "*Ten'shun*!" he barked. God, what a bark the man had. You could practically picture the whole of World War II from it. "Things are going to be different now in this outfit, men. No more fiddle-fucking around …"

As I, for one, suddenly saw a chunky being, ear flaps dancing, stout legs pumping, coming out of the gym door and heading hell bent for the far reaches. He still had that goofy smile on his face. He caught my eye and gave me a look as if we were both understood what was happening. He fled behind Sergeant Weldon, out of his sight. What had got into Half Bright? I couldn't believe he could run that fast. Before I could think more I saw a weirder sight. Kelso was flying out behind him in nothing but his olive green drawers that came down to his knees. So that was why he slept with all those blankets over him. He didn't sleep with his clothes on as the rest of us did, as normal human beings would.

"Hit the deck, men!" Kelso screamed over his shoulder, his legs pumping away. "The son of a bitch is going to blow!"

I saw a tiny tongue of orange work its way outside our window above the gym, searching for somewhere to go. It came to me, idly at first, that our ammunition was stored up there in the room beside our own. Those of us in the small room never really thought about its proximity. Why should we? We were in the army. Ammunition had to be stored somewhere. Someone was in charge, someone in a supposedly responsible position had thought up where it should go. It had to be stored somewhere. The price we paid for escaping the barracks and having a room of our own was that we slept next to a load of howitzer shells and clips of bullets. Someone had a key to the room and authority to open it. Occasionally I heard footsteps outside going in, and muffled talk. I didn't lie in bed at night worrying about all that ammo next to me. I might lie in bed at night dreaming of sexy women or dreaming about the boat that would take me back home, but never a concern of what lay inches from my head next door. I was 18. I was immortal. I had thought up Special Services as a way to get away from others and be on my own.

"Sergeant," I said, on the parade ground, my voice slightly rising above a whisper because we weren't to talk, especially at Attention, "there's ammo up there. I think a fire is starting up there."

It turned out that Half Bright had run out of kerosene, could not get the stove fire going, and had thrown on a splash of gasoline. Or maybe he couldn't tell the difference between kerosene and gasoline. That was the conclusion some came to later. Sergeant Weldon, our new Top Kick, his first day on the job, became highly irritated at this series of interruptions at Roll Call, scowling at me who dared to whisper in line and cursing at the men who stood at attention in front of him. That man who'd run out in his underpants in freezing weather was crazy as a loon or thinks he can pull a prank in my company. By God, he'd ream some asses for all these shenanigans when he had time to sort things out. He hadn't been through the Battle of the Bulge and the Huertgen Forest for nothing. Then he rolled his eyes to look where those in front of him were looking. Standing straight, he saw the small tongue of orange suddenly burst into a fire ball, sending glass flying. *Shit oh dear! Take cover, men!*

We took off, M-1's in hand, zigzagging bent-over as bullets and shells whizzed by. It was as if the Red Army had now decided to come down. I ended up behind a plywood barrack, peeking around the corner to see the flames grow and the fireworks increase.

Mixed in with the pop pop pop of bullets came the wham wham wham of shells, and then the finale of a grand bang, followed by a moment of silence. I looked at a soldier beside me I didn't recognize and he looked at me. We nodded at each other, being quiet for some reason, and inched our way toward the pyre. The skeleton of the once grand Japanese army gym stood like a bombed out structure from World War II. Edges of it glowed and in the center low flames flickered. As we got nearer and nearer, cautiously moving forward, more in wonder than from any curiosity, hunched over, I saw where I guess my small room once had been. Jesus, I had just pulled myself out of the sack there a few minutes ago! Wow! Ain't that something? Wonder if anything is left? Then the pop of a bullet sent me flying back to behind the barrack. At the same time came Sergeant Weldon's bark, *"All men stay clear of building until further orders, God damn it!"* He didn't have to tell us again. No one then, or later, was called on the carpet for causing the fire. No one up above seemed to care. No one had taken a bullet, no head was blown off. Later we found nicks and holes in the concrete of old Japanese buildings around us and through the boards of the stinky latrine where at least some fresh air had a chance to come in.

Half-Bright kept running and was never seen again. Kelso returned holding a blanket around himself, bitching. All I know is that I had to wear what I had on until the Supply Room, which was skimpily supplied, could come up with something to outfit me in. Somehow I was a difficult fit and the fatigue pants that the Supply Room had to offer came down to an inch or two above my ankles and the waist could be stretched a half foot from my belly. But requisitions went out and in a week I was rewarded with a brand new set of clothing, as if I'd just joined up. I even got a new-issue fur-lined Parker that no one else had. The Army was giving me a treat, I guess. All my Christmas gifts from home had gone up in smoke, all the letters, pictures, paperbacks, the works. I had to barge in one of the jerry-built barracks and find an empty bunk. What I found turned out to be next to the door where arctic air blew in with every entrance and exit. I didn't know enough to be glad reveille had saved me and I was alive.

After a slim garden-type looking hose was somehow brought into action a day or two later and the remains doused with water, and after the smoke and acrid smell went away, a Lieutenant with a cheery smile arrived bouncing in a Jeep with a clipboard and a camera. It was spring weather by that time. He wanted to gather evidence of the explosion and fire and he wanted to make a list of all personal items I had lost and their relative value. I was given to understand that the Government was going to pay me for what I had lost. Amazing. He said it would. He very carefully wrote items down and we thought about the value of each. Often the value I gave something would not be enough for him. He made me reconsider, sometimes doubling what I had thought. For instance, the price tag on a Kodak that folded out like an accordion. I could hardly believe it. The Army cared! A little over a year after the *Enola Gray* dropped the A-bomb on Hiroshima. We had come ashore at Normandy and nearly leveled Berlin. Here now came a Lieutenant taking down items lost in a fire. I half suspected that it was either a mistake or that rules out of nowhere required it or something. There was a place for me to sign on an official document. I did so, and the Lieutenant screwed the top on the fountain pen, put it away, and said compensation would come through the mail to my home address in Tennessee. I still see his cheery smile and the carefulness with which he looked over my shoulder to make sure I signed on the proper line, the authority with which he screwed on the top of his fountain pen and put it away. If I hadn't known better I would have thought it was all pretense. He didn't know what he was doing. The Army didn't know what it was doing. I never heard from the Government one way or the other. It's been over half a century.

But I did hear from Red, a gangly lopsided corporal from the South who handed out the mail, whose accent you could cut with a knife. "Here's one for you," he said, presenting an envelop, the handwriting on which caused my heart to race and a blush to come to my cheeks although I hadn't read a thing inside it. Just that she had written to me was enough. The words were drawn in neatly, small letters, and with authority and confidence. It came from the girl I had never kissed, one I had irresistibly fallen in love with in high school. The handwriting had found its way, upon request, beneath her yearbook picture scarcely a year before, telling me, "Johnny, you're going to go far" (oh, boy, how true) and that I was one of her "fav-o-rites". God, that girl knew how to get to you. Just writing, me getting a letter from her unexpectedly was enough to start the trembles. She didn't have much to say ("I'm really enjoying it here in college. It's all so new. The girls here in the dorm are so nice.")

The girl I had never kissed was thousands of miles and another era away. She was purity with a certain erotic quality attached and someone that had absolutely nothing to do with my life in the army. She was everything the army was not. She represented home. It made me want to get to know, pal around with, someone with the "values." She and the thought of home brought on that wish. But someone with "values" was not the easiest thing to find in the U.S. army. I stumbled across Lawler who carried those qualities like a beacon. He was a high school graduate. He came from a small town in Ohio. His mother baked pies. His father had worked for the same company all his life since he had started work. Meals were on time. He professed to being a Presbyterian. Along with his American bone fides there were hints of things perhaps off kilter. He had thick wet lips that he was always moving and often applying a chap stick to. He had a ready smile and a deep chuckle. In my new quarters he dropped by, plopping down on my bunk. Shortly after listing the dishes his mother cooked back home, he said, out of the blue, "I had intercourse with my teacher back home."

"Yeah," I said, trying to catch my breath.

"Yeah. I didn't want to, you know. We were in her car. She was giving me a lift home after school and she parked a block away from my house and before I knew it we were having sexual intercourse. I was just devastated."

"You were?" Was he kidding?

"Yeah. I didn't have her in class then and I did my best to avoid her."

"You did?"

"Yeah. But after a school function one night she gave me another lift home and parked a block away. She put a rubber on for me. I didn't want to do it."

"And then you did it?"

"Yeah." And he smiled wetly with those big sensual lips that were chapped from the cold in Korea. "Listen," he said, maddingly not going on, "there's this family from my hometown and the father is on some kind of government junket here in Seoul. He's living in a house, right here in Korea. It's an open invitation. Want to pay him a visit?"

For some reason I wasn't enthusiastic. Maybe it was the respectability of a family friend suddenly transplanted to where it smelled of garlic and there were crater holes in the roads. I hadn't joined the army for respectability, and I had trouble thinking of a civilian, this man, in a house with running water and heat when I hadn't had a shower in several months. We went. It looked like a regular American suburban home plunked down on the outskirts of Seoul. I gathered that civilian government workers had a completely different way of life, had escaped army discipline and regulations. They acted as if they held superior positions and wore olive drab and khakis that carried no sign of the military or rank. The family friend was chipper, and after a few words about Lawler's family back home, fell into talk about Syngman Rhee and the political scene, the economics of the region, and the USO – all of which I half listened to with the same kind of smile Lawler generally carried. We drank Coca Colas and then Lawler and I caught a ride back to base on a two-and-a-half.

Lawler never told me anything more about the teacher he had had sexual intercourse with. I kept hoping though. I told him a few more times about the girl I had never kissed, raising her to girlfriend status but not confessing I had never kissed her. I mooned over her, blushed at the first sight of her coming down the hall in high school. She brought on big emotions and thoughts that were pure. Keeping her pure was the only way I knew of being in love. I see her squatting beside her locker, bringing something out. I see her white silk blouse buttoned to the top. She wears saddle oxfords with brilliant white socks turned down above her ankles. She smiles up angelically at me, as if we're in a play. Both of us are playing parts and going by a script. Now I am in the army acting like a soldier, my real self left behind. I'm playing another part.

One late afternoon outside of Lawler's hovering straight-laced presence, I saw Red coming around delivering mail. He paused, shuffling the letters. He let it be known that he had somehow contracted a few girls to take on any who were willing.

"Who, when, and where's the place? . . . How much?"

Red talked out of the side of his mouth, rifling the letters in his hands. The place was to be on military grounds but well away from the Orderly Room. Red would do all the arranging and slip the girls in. I wasn't sure what he was getting out of it except maybe to get one of the girls free. He liked being an entrepreneur. So we ended up in a room on the far reaches of the compound. We could smell the garlic and a whiff of an oil drum fire. Not much noise outside, a rumble of a truck from somewhere, a door screeched open, then banged shut, but no human voices. I could see the moon outside a window that had no shade. In a few minutes the girls would come. They would know what to do. Would I? Every second counted, and I fought to get aroused before the first peek of them came. And why was I thinking of a bevy of girls. I was the only one in the room. Maybe Red had stashed other G.I.'s down the hall in other rooms. But here I was, alone in a room with a harsh electric blub hanging down from overhead, waiting and feeling my heart pump. I must get aroused or all of Red's arrangements would go for naught.

I had not become accustomed to irony as I would later, and marvel at it, but the fact was that usually, 24 hours a day, I was horney. Now I called on nature to come through and nothing happened. *The girls were coming!* I heard Red's voice and whisper. I tried any number of scenarios and then, as I looked at the moon, I brought out the trump card. I brought forth the girl I had never kissed and had her pose with juice running down her leg. Please forgive me, Lord. This is an emergency. A black-eyed girl in traditional Korean grab, white blouse and black skirt, opened the door shyly and I caught a glimpse of Red checking off a name on a clipboard outside. The door closed. I had given him a carton of cigarettes earlier for the girl's visit so all that remained now was consummation of business. I pointed to myself, said my name, then pointed to her. I thought she might roll her eyes and flirt as Miss Kim had done on Bung Chung Street. I was trying to be polite about it all as if the furtherest thought in my mind was fucking her. She said nothing but in her black eyes was a look of total crippling fear. I was too preoccupied with my own fear to have noticed it before. I see those eyes now. They will not leave me. I might have been just as afraid but there was a big difference. I represented the American army and was in a seat of power and God knows what stories went around about us. Had Red waylaid her in Seoul and brought her here or was he in cahoots with an all-too-smiling Korean go-between with girls at the ready? We'd heard that the Japanese had set up whorehouses for their horney troops, stocked with Korean girls, so maybe this girl had continued on with us in the trade. But she acted too shy, too afraid to be an old hand at it. But what was the use of thinking? Just putting on a rubber – or trying to – was enough to set action in place and change the scenario. She who had no name looked up at the ceiling. It was over, whatever we did, and she was out the door.

Days were marked by events that had no precedent. Take private Lipshitz from Yonkers. I felt pity for him as I did the black-eyed girl, carrying around a last name that always got a snigger when roll was called. I see him now, as I see the black-eyed girl with no name. I see his boots with his fatigue pants tucked in or held by a tied rubber, issued for another purpose, which we all did. I can't remember if he was neat or not. Something tells me he tried for neatness and to do what was expected or commanded. But he was no soldier. And that gave him symphony, at least from me. He didn't talk much and carried a kind of pained, mystified look on his face. He may have been asking himself what he was doing here. What he was doing was riding out each morning in a two-and-a-half with his squad, bouncing up and down, and then supervising Koreans to fix something – a partially washed out road that needed gravelling or pot holes that needed filling. He got endless Care packages from home. I remember that, but I can't recall what they contained or if he shared with others. He didn't seem to have made friends in the company, but he sure got Care packages sent his way. He had blue eyes and he walked stiffly. No athlete Lipshitz. No hail fellow, well met. He was a number, as all of us were, with dog tags around our necks that proved it, something we never took off. But somewhere back in the States someone must have loved him as Lipshitz because those packages from home kept piling up beside his bunk.

I've wondered how they took the news back home. I'd delivered telegrams during the War because of the man power shortage and I'd left my bike sprawled beside the pavement and made myself walk up to a front door. I had on a Western Union cap that meant I carried a message of some import. The gray-haired, hawk-faced woman who hesitated to greet me or take the envelope in my hand kept moaning, No, no, no. Her daughter who was a couple of grades behind me in school stood behind her, embarrassed. She had a weak confused smile on her face, not having an example at hand for what to do. Her brother, the gray-haired woman's son, was fighting in Europe. The telegram which I was forced by the rules to have the mother sign reported that her son had been killed. It may have said, "paid the ultimate sacrifice," or something like that, anything to soften it, but what was fact was that he had been killed.

I couldn't help but run over in my mind the home of Lipshitz where the telegram was sure to come and where no more Care packages would leave. In my mind I see his parents as elderly although there was no reason to think so. I see his mother come to the door in a smock and apron, looking tired and forlorn, wiping her hands on a dish towel. I see his father in suspenders, reading the evening paper, looking up as the messenger rings the bell. That's as far as I go. And I see Lipshitz always alive, in his sad-looking boots, a goofy crooked smile on his face. He would never get the GI Bill of Rights. He wouldn't get to go home.

Neither would Gonzales, a rotund Private First Class with a lively smile, unlike Lipshitz's mournful one. Gonzales was a fuck up and unapologetic about it. He didn't seem to mind the Army but he didn't intend to get ahead in it. That exactly fit my point of view although I tried to avoid being a fuck up; mostly I was successful. Gonzales never was. He missed reveille. On KP he couldn't peel a potato. His rifle couldn't pass inspection. He never got a letter. But he remains of good cheer in my mind. "Hey, Gonzales, you've really fucked-up this time," a sergeant would say, more in sorrow than in anger. Once he shit his pants on a frigid winter night. Too deep in sleep to get up and go to the latrine in the sub-zero night. In the morning: "Jesus, what's that smell?" Gonzales just smiled and went about his business, unhurried to claim responsibility or to clean up the mess. But strangely enough he was a pretty good soldier. He was the first to try to get a truck mired in mud moving again. He was ready to climb to an observation tower on guard duty. When his squad went out on assignment after a storm to clear an area a broken wire was sighted lying across a road. The driver didn't want to pass over it. No one volunteered to investigate. Finally Gonzales climbed down with no one ordering him to and picked up the wire. "What's the matter, you guys chicken?" Those were his last words. He was dead in a second.

Botsford was another disaster case, but you'd never know it at first glance. Where Gonzales had been untidy to say the least, Botsford was fastidious. Average height, clean looks, clean shaven, he wore metal framed glasses that were never smudged. His voice was even without a trace of accent. I never saw him laugh. He was steely-eyed behind those glasses. I pictured him as a choir boy back where he came from and someone I could bring into my own buttoned-up home as I could clean-cut Lawler. The number was not large in that department and I was in no hurry to mix Army and home. I wanted to return and sit in the living room reading Charles Dickens, drinking a glass of milk, and not worrying about someone coming in and disturbing the peace.

But Botsford kept doing something that no one else did. He kept catching the clap as if he was out to break the world's record (which he may have done.). Usually you kept quiet about catching it. A joke went: "I've never had the clap and what's more I don't want to have it again." One thought was that if he caught it a ridiculous number of times he would get discharged and sent home. But the Army didn't like to be outfoxed. There was a clap shack set up for VD victims. It was in a compound all its own. Once in, you couldn't mingle with anyone from the outside. No one wanted to visit you there anyhow, or if you were inside yourself you certainly didn't yearn for visitors. It was laughable that anyone could even consider visiting a buddy there. Once inside, no communication with the outside. There could have been barbed wire around it for all I know. Let out, it was as if you wore a scarlet letter. You mumbled and lied about where you'd been. You went to the clap shack to be isolated and put in shame and almost as an afterthought, cured. But everyone knew where you'd been. You didn't broadcast it. It was not as if you'd taken a bullet and deserved the Purple Heart.

The strange thing about Botsford was that he came back each time as if it was just a little bad luck and didn't matter in the long run. He was edging near a world record of the number of times a person could catch the clap and live. Everyone was astounded. He became a legend. "I hear Botsford's come down with it again. He's caught it something like 30 times. How can a man keep doing that?" It wasn't that high a number, but high enough. Maybe he only came down with it nine or ten times but just catching it once and being cured was usually enough for any man. It was a wicked strain of the clap, too, more lethal than its form in the States. Maybe he worked in a bout of syphilis for good measure, too. A few in company had caught it. Botsford would sit before an Army psychiatrist, pale, all seriousness, cool as a cucumber, and say he hadn't used "protection," wasn't thinking, wasn't going to do it again. He'd learned his lesson. Something like that to get him off the hook. To us, he said, "I can't stand using a rubber. It kills it for me." Before authority, before the psychiatrist, he looked as trustworthy as an Eagle Scout. Who would ever think he would go out and catch it again. I wondered where he found the women. He was sure getting around, and they eventually gave it to him, not the other way around because I was dead certain he didn't fool around if he knew he had it. I was standing in the latrine next to him once when he said, in resignation, and deep sorrow, "Shit oh dear, look at that. I got it again."

I guess the brass wanted to break him. They figured he was catching it because he wanted out of Korea. Hell, everyone wanted out, even the Koreans wanted out. But the brass wasn't going to oblige him. They had enough penicillin to treat the whole XXIV Corps, so good luck, Charley. Each time he came down with it he would shake his head and swear this was absolutely the last time they would see him. Or he told them something. Then he would go out and come down with it again. He was in the clap shack when our unit moved to another location and I never heard what happened to him.

In winter, after the room over the gym burned down and I was back on barracks life and guard duty I came down with a cough that wouldn't go away. It got deeper and deeper in my chest and my face stayed flush. Finally I was too weak to climb aboard the truck for guard duty. I had been made to understand in the Army that you couldn't go on sick call unless near death. I hardly realized that you could go on sick call. My father who worked for the Southern Railway never took a sick day off in the fifty years he worked there. Maybe he was never sick. I thought you just had to tough it out. I was in the Army. Did the troops that went ashore on D-Day or who fought in the Argonne take a day off sick? I couldn't help being trapped in the mind-set of World War II. Then I stumbled to the Orderly Room where our new First Sergeant, the battle hardened soldier of Normandy who had been an officer over there, a captain, Sergeant Weldon, looked up at me from his desk with narrowed eyes.

"What's the matter with you, soldier?"

"I don't know. I'm sick, I guess." My voice was so hoarse it was as if someone else was speaking. I didn't try to disguise it.

"Where you 'spose to be?"

"Guard duty."

"Go to the Dispensary. Go with him, Brooklyn. If his temperature isn't well over a hundred get him back on the truck." He returned to papers on his desk.

"Thank you, Sergeant," I said, and he didn't answer.

Anyone from Brooklyn got called "Brooklyn" from time to time. It was a given. Leftkovitz was among three others from that borough, and he didn't seem to relish being branded with the name. I came from Tennessee and saw what he meant. It was before Tennessee Williams gave the name some distinction and class. I followed in the wake of Leftkovitz' pear shaped figure to a small compact building that was neater and cleaner than others and had an antiseptic scent that both frightened and assured me. Silver medical instruments lay about and steam rose from some device somewhere and it was warmer than in the barracks. Here was where the sick came. Leftkovitz hovered by me as a thermometer went under my tongue. I saw that he had fuzz on his cheeks and no hint of a beard. He looked even younger than me. "How is it out in the field?" he said. I pointed to the thermometer, and he said, "Oh, yeah. Sorry. Forgot. I was just wondering what it's like being out there in the open all day?"

What it's like I wanted to tell him, if the thermometer hadn't been there, is that you're out there in the middle of nowhere freezing your balls off doing something that is absolutely of no consequence. He went on, "I'm going bats stuck in that Orderly Room. I wish I'd never learned how to type."

The thermometer was pulled out by corporal I'd seen occasionally in the chow line taking on a superior attitude, nearly sniffing the air, but not knowing what he did. Now I realized. He was a Medic. Wonder how he got such a cushiony job? "Jesus," he said, reading the thermometer.

"What is it?" Leftkovitz said, looking over his shoulder. He was really a jumpy guy. "What does it say?"

The Medic didn't deign to answer. He called, "Captain Leonard, could you come over here for a second please?"

Captain Leonard ambled over. He was thin and stoop shouldered and had gone to Yale. He seemed displeased with everything he faced and couldn't wait to go back Stateside. But through it all he had the look of a doctor, was a doctor, and I knew he would do his duty. I had the chance to check in the beautiful dispensary and sleep in a bed with clean sheets. He read the thermometer.

"What is it?" Leftkovitz wanted to know.

He didn't deign to even look at him. "Go tell your First Sergeant that I'm checking this man in. He's relieved of duty." Thank you, Lord. Leftkovitz waved and was gone.

I was taken through a door and into another room with two rows of beds. It was not grand but it was a sight for sore eyes. I would soon be snug in one of those beds and I would sleep and sleep and sleep. Several patients, if you could call them that, were under the covers and presented a condescending smile or two. If you were a newcomer anywhere in the Army you know the condescending or disinterested look of a veteran if only for a day or two will give a newcomer. I was out of my fatigues in no time, into a gown, and under the covers getting warm. I was back in a white frame home on West Watauga Avenue in Johnson City, Tennessee. My mother would soon bring me hot potato soup. My dad would bring me the afternoon paper. Then I saw Aberdeen lying back, knees up, a few bunks over. He was talking, telling a fresh group of listeners about making out with a nurse aboard the troop ship coming over. I had heard it before but could hear it again. It was like a familiar bedtime story where details might change but the essential story remained. Before the nurse had been of Swedish extraction. Now she was French and had been a bit actress in the movies before nurse's training. How a French bit player in movies could turn herself into being a troopship nurse no one thought to ask. No one, as had happened before, questioned Aberdeen's veracity. He then began a ramble about how the Koreans would steal the socks off your feet and I began to drift away. I was awakened by a flashlight pointed at my face. I barely made out the Medic with the superior air behind the beam. "Here, take these."

He shook three aspirins in my hand and then gave me a glass of water to wash them down with after which he took my temperature. I didn't ask what it read. I didn't care. All I knew was that I was under clean sheets and no reveille in the morning. I went back to sleep, somewhat angry at the intrusion, thinking they should know I was sick. A couple of hours later the flashlight beam came in my face once again. Three pills went in one palm, a glass of water in the other. It continued that way until the light of day lit up the room. I saw the Medic go through the routine with Aberdeen who seemed to be able to sleep through the taking of the pills. His mouth came open, his eyes shut. He continued snoring. He was a veteran of the infirmary I supposed. And the Army, I suspected, woke us up through the night regardless of the pills, medicinal benefits, or what we claimed was wrong with us, just to weed out malingerers.

When the light of day broke through I was shaken awake and told to put my clothes on. I was going to have X-rays taken. Pneumonia was suspected. I had no fear of it. In fact, I felt immortal and pneumonia sounded like a minor inconvenience. I would go to a serious hospital perhaps, maybe Japan, and leave behind guard duty and the new First Sergeant. It wasn't as good as being shot in combat and feeling like a hero but it would do. So, fatigues and field jacket on loosely, boots untied, I sat shivering in the back of a two-and-a-half, along with four or five other soldiers in similar distress, and bounced up the road inhaling dust and coughing up a storm, eyes watering, before ending up at a big brick building near a rice paddy. Inside, shirt off, bare chest slumped forward, I went through the X-ray ritual. "Deep breath. Hold it. Breath." When the Medic came out with a large envelope that held the results, I said, "Have I got anything?"

He didn't say. He said, "Take this back with you." Captain Leonard, the doctor with the Yale pedigree, looked them over carefully when I got back, perhaps showing that he was a conscientious doctor. I coughed, to let him know I wasn't a malingerer. "You haven't got anything," he said dolefully. "Stay in the infirmary a day or two more. Till your cough gets better."

For the next few days I watched some I recognized enter and leave, most of us there presented with a flashlight in the face and aspirins in the hand through the night. I thought about the girl I had never kissed back home. Wonder if she ever got sick? Confined to bed I lost the sense of night and day but my fever went down and the cough left my chest and before I knew it I was pulling on in my fatigues and heading for the Orderly Room, back for duty.

The new First Sergeant, Sergeant Weldon, raised an eyebrow at me and said nothing. Leftkovitz from Brooklyn greeted me with a squeaky adolescent voice, jumping around. "How was it in there? You feel all right now? Good to see you back!"

Guard duty was posted for the following week, all neatly typed. As Company Clerk, Leftkovitz had typed it up. He was a good typist and so was I. My mother had bought me an Underwood Noiseless Typewriter when I was 13 and a typing skill that followed was something that just happened, nothing to get me a job or to be useful in a commercial way. The Army had never asked if I knew how to type. In fact, it had never asked me much of anything once I had passed the physical and raised my right hand. I never thought of typing and the army going together in any way. I felt it somewhat obscene. To me the army meant shouldering arms and going overseas. Guard duty in sub zero weather with little sleep came as a shock. I did wonder sometimes how someone, say, became a cook. Did someone or something somewhere mark you down as having cooking potential?

Leftkovitz followed me around, not like a puppy but close. He followed me to the barracks, looking up to me, figurately I imagined and literally. I was 6'2" and he was down there somewhere looking up, a grin on his fuzz cheeked face. His patter went on and on, in a good natured way and I half-listened and was secretly pleased by his interest. No one else had. Where did I hail from? Tennessee. Wow. He was from Brooklyn as if I didn't know. You probably have no trouble out in the field. You must have hunted and used a gun before. I then got a hint of why he was interested in me. He was sick of being behind a desk in the Orderly Room, probably sick of the First Sergeant Weldon. I leveled with him. I couldn't get over that fuzz on his plump cheeks and his nervousness over nothing.

MY KOREA – A YEAR LOST IN SERVICE 1946-47

"It's really rough out in the field. I nearly got pneumonia, you know. You're out in all weather and your tail bounces up and down in the two-and-a-half until you're screaming and the final thing is that you really don't know what you're doing out there. You're watching Koreans fix bridges or something. You could die. That's all."

"Beats the Orderly Room. You're out there. You're a group and you carry M-1's. You're doing what the army does. You're a team. I'm sitting behind a desk the same way I could be in Brooklyn. I didn't have to enlist to be doing what I'm doing. I'm getting no experience! I'll go home with no experience!"

"Be grateful. Some experiences you can do without."

"I haven't even been drunk. Have you been drunk yet?"

"Sure," I lied. He was looking up to me as some sort of veteran of experience, me of 18, who didn't need to shave, who was desperately in love with a girl I had never kissed. I had lain on top of a Korean woman who raised her black skirt for all of ten seconds but I didn't want to go into that. "Sometime I'll show you how to get drunk," I said.

"Let's go to the EM Club tonight," he said. "If you haven't anything better to do."

"Sure, why not. There's nothing to getting drunk." That said, I lay on my bunk, hands behind my head, and watched his roly poly frame walk away, a sly anticipating smile on his cherubic face. That evening he was in the Club before I got there. Smoke as thick as concrete covered all. Guffaws and curses rose and fell and soldiers in heavy boots stood before a plank board placed over two upended oil drums. We warmed ourselves over oil drums, took shits in them and now we drank over them. Drinks and beer cans lay on the boards. I spotted Leftkovitz through the haze. Although it was stifling from the warmth of massed bodies he was swinging his arms back and forth as if cold. His face lit up when he saw me and he immediately made room for me at what passed for a bar. "O.K., let's start. I'm ready."

I thought it over now that we actually stood in the EM Club where the sharp bite of alcohol rose in the air. "Are you really sure? Heck, this is your idea, I want you to know. I'm not trying to talk you into anything."

"I'm ready, I tell you. Order 'em up and let's get crackin'. I want to know what it's like to be drunk." He was rubbing his hands together and taking on a Southern accent that would never pass.

"But why haven't you tried it before?"

"I don't know. Scared, I guess. Drinking wasn't big back home. But you come from Tennessee, man. Hell, there's drinking down there, podner. Don't tell me there's not. You're going to be my guide!"

I wasn't used to flattery and immediately felt proud of experience and knowledge I didn't have. I didn't mind Leftkovitz taking liberties with my accent, and I didn't want to let him down. He was looking up to me. Hell, I was supposed to have been around. "Fine," I said. I ordered two bourbons and ginger from the GI bartender behind the plank bar as if I had been doing it all my life. I had watched others ordering the same concoction. I even took on something of a weary air, too sophisticated and jaded for words and pushed funny money out nonchalantly to pay for it. I took a taste. The ginger ale covered the harshness of the Bourbon. Leftkovitz gulped it down. I remembered seeing him drink a Coke in the Orderly Room once. It reminded me of that. "Don't feel a thing," he said. He reared back, gazed around the club, and squared his shoulders. "There's nothing to this drinking. Let's have another."

I got him another, none for myself. I watched him, fascinated. A silly grin remained on his beardless face as he downed his second one in a few gulps. I waited as if listening to a ticking clock, waiting for the bomb to go off. Maybe I should warn him about having any more but I knew little about the process of alcoholic intake on the human body. I was learning along with Leftkovitz, the difference being that he was more the Guiney pig than I was. "Hey, I'm getting drunk!" he shouted, but I could tell he was pretending. He was acting. I got him another refill but this time it took more than a few gulps to get it down. I shook my head when the bartender nodded toward me. None for me. This was Lelfkovitz's show. Finally he was bouncing around, eyes rolling, talking to the four walls. "Hey, this is getting drunk. I'm getting drunk with my old drinking buddy from Tennessee!"

Before I knew it I had an arm around his shoulder and was leading him out. He really did have to be supported. Others in the Club, some veterans from World War II, hardly gave us a glance as if they were disgusted or had seen this once too often. The sharp air outside had no effect. He kept babbling about how he was drunk, that this was what it was all about. *Hot dog!* I got him to the Quonset hut and onto his bunk. He passed out with his boots on and I noted that they had not lost their shine. It was an Orderly Room shine that had seen no service in the field.

In the morning he showed up in the chow line, paler than usual but a smile on this face, a little weaker now but still a smile. "Man, we tied one on last night, didn't we?"

"Yeah. Sure did. How you feeling?"

"Fine, really fine." But he only took coffee in the chow line and only a sip of that. I didn't take any coffee. I didn't drink it in the army. I yearned for whole milk that was never there and peanut butter on soft white bread and a hard apple. That was my addiction which the army was doing its best to cure me of. I didn't smoke but once in awhile bummed a cigarette to pretend. Leftkovitz actually kept a pack of Camels handy but he didn't inhale. You could tell the smokers by how deeply they took the smoke in and how relieved and satisfied they became as a gray stream issued through lips and noses. Cartons of cigarettes were available at practically no cost in funny money and could be used by those who didn't require it personally as barter for haircuts and laundering and sex.

Addictions answered overpowering needs in the army. Tobacco offered the idea of camaraderie and relief from the stress, a path to bogus calmness. Drink offered a ticket to another world, one away from the unbearable sights and psyches, of sergeants barking orders and temperatures freezing the hair on your balls, living with night sweats and longing with all your heart to go home. Or maybe you were just born to smoke and drink and go crazy and the army was there to accommodate. Red the Drunk, as distinguished from our other "Reds," was a Skid Row drunk and a WWII vet who generally lived somewhere in our Quonset hut but I was never quite sure where because he moved around like a nomad. No one wanted to sleep beside him, in our Quonset hut or elsewhere. Sometimes he was there, sometimes he was gone. He was in the stockade or he was AWOL or he was in the infirmary (like me) and his bunk changed. You knew he was in your Quonset when he carried on a conversation with himself through the night with an occasional song thrown in. Besides Skidrow Red there was Mailman Red and Quartermaster Red. Anyone who had red hair was in danger of being signaled out. It was like Brooklyn. Skidrow Red was the first to discover, and the only one to drink as far as anyone knew, a cloudy Korean product you could set on fire. He sang through the night after drinking a bottle of it. Where he got it no one knew. How he got through World War II and into Korea no one knew. I learned that the army wanted warm bodies to swell the ranks and didn't ask too many questions. I shouldn't have been so proud to be accepted into its ranks, but I was.

And I was on Guard Duty the night after reporting back for duty. It didn't help to tell myself that someone had to do it, someone had to climb to a guard tower, lugging an M-1, and stay still and watchful for much of the night. Waiting for the Russians or the North Koreans to descend I supposed and certainly waiting for my relief that was always late. I thought about the girl I had never kissed and hungered for a hot buttered biscuit.

What I got the next day was Leftkovitz who ambled in the Guard Room and asked what I did on Guard Duty, what was the experience like? He was excused of course since he held the essential job of Company Clerk and the First Sergeant needed him at his beck and call 24 hours a day. He was exempt from Guard and KP duties. Sweet. "Guard Duty," I said, "is the pits."

"Listen," he said, not very good at listening himself, "what if we traded jobs? I go out on the line and pull guard and you be the Company Clerk?"

"Just stay inside and be cooped up with the First Sergeant all day?" I said. I didn't want to seem too eager but my heart beat fast. "I don't know."

"Listen, let's give it a try. Let's go talk to him."

So us two recent high school grads went to face a veteran of the Battle of the Bulge and the storming of Normandy. Sergeant Weldon looked us over and didn't smile when we told him the news. "You unhappy with me here, Brooklyn?"

"No, certainly not, Sergeant," Leftkovitz said to the man from Texas. "It's just that I'm going back Stateside in a couple of months and I'd like to have the experience of being on the line before I go. This is my last chance."

"Your last chance of enjoying guard duty and KP, Leftkovitz?" I thought I noticed a twinkle in the Sergeant's eyes.

"I'm a soldier, Sergeant. I don't only want the memory of sitting behind a typewriter and being out of the rain. No disrespect, Sergeant."

"And you," he said turning to me in a military manner. "You want a cushiony job and to get out of the rain? Is that it?"

"No, Sergeant," I lied. "I think the army can better use me if I use my typing skills instead of being out on the line," which was the truth.

Sgt. Weldon turned away and cleared his throat. As far as I knew he had two forms of expression: irritation and extreme irritation. Now he just seemed disgruntled. If this was what the army was coming to, so be. "O.K.," he said, looking at Leftkovitz, the instigator. "we'll give it try. But don't come running back to me, Brooklyn, if you change your mind. This is it." He turned to me, freezing me in place. "You satisfied?"

"Yes, I am."

I lost contact with Leftkovitz but not the sight of him. He went to another Quonset and I only caught glimpses of him as when a truck came barreling in from the line and he tenderly lowered himself covered in dust or his pale face was revealed within an over sized helmet when spotted walking in a daze after just getting off guard duty at dawn. Leftkovitz. He was determined to not miss out on anything. And he was just as determined to shuck it all and get back home. A day or two before the ship that was to take him home docked at Inchon a strange sight appeared in the Quonset doorway. It was an American civilian in loose fitting civilian clothes and pork pie hat. The weather was warmish, not the heretofore brutal cold, and he seemed to have on an Hawaiian shirt. It was, by God, Leftkovitz. Surely he was going to get court marshaled for that. But how in the world had he come by the duds? He wouldn't say. He tried to act normally, as normally as someone we had known as Private First Class Leftkovitz, but we had trouble drinking him in in a pork pie hat and Hawaiian shirt. He took a few puffs on a cigarette which he didn't inhale, dropped it, ground it out with his foot (a neat civilian slipper), lifted his hand in a sort of salute, and walked away. I never saw him again. It was among the many hallucinary sights I carried back with me to the States, one without an answer. Had he carried those clothes with him somehow in his duffle bag, through countless inspections? Had he stolen them from someone – but who? The sight of him in civvies, when all around was a sea of olive green uniforms, cheered my heart. I felt good all over. Someday we'd all be dressed that way. And the army itself would turn into a dream, as incomprehensible as Leftkovitz was now in Pork Pie hat.

*   *   *

Oh, I longed for home! I thought about the girl I'd never kissed, and found myself early in the evening in the EM club. I saw familiar faces from the Company but no one I could sidle up to and pretend I knew what I was doing as I had with Leftkovitz. Everyone was getting bombed as it seemed they had been for ages, smoke blanketing all, and all had someone to talk to but me. When the EM bartender looked me in the eye, I pointed to a drink before someone down the two plank bar and soon had a ginger and seven in hand. I cupped it the way others were doing and brought it slowly to my lips. I struck what I considered a world weary expression and looked at the door as if expecting someone. I had heard army drunks growling about busted marriages, terrible relatives, jobs gone sour, growling to themselves. Lefkovitz, poor sod, had growled about a younger sister who had got all the family's attention. I looked for something to growl about. All alone at the bar I thought of the girl I had never kissed – her large widely spaced eyes, her concerned frown when anyone tried to explain something, her cheerleader's body (she had been a cheerleader), her purity, a whole Sears & Roeback catalogue of enticements. And then the one who had claimed her in high school muscled in my thoughts: Daffy Duck who was now stationed down in Pusan.

Someone from our Company C now magically had me by the elbow, guiding me out the door and stumbling toward our Quonset. I felt required to do what I thought drunk people did, what Leftkovitz had done, what Skidrow Red did all the time even when at Shoulder Arms. Inside the squad's Quonset I stood before the pot belly stove and addressed a poker game, men lying on their bunks, a few cleaning rifles or writing home and I brought them to attention. I caught their amused looks and felt I was doing a good job. I was making an ass out of myself, and they were delighted. I said, "He took her away from me. He did. He's down in Pusan far from the 38th Parallel where he'll be when they run over us up here. Nothing will happen to him. He'll go back to her. He'll go back to her Mona Lisa smile and those big brown eyes and I'll be a dead cooked goose up here in this God forsaken outpost not far from the 38th. He's Daffy Duck and I'm a Cooked Goose." I don't know where I came up with this shit but I screamed it out until I lost my voice and fell back on my bunk as if pole axed. I remember the words from that screed to this day. Maybe it was because I pretended more about being drunk than being drunk. But I did get a taste of a liberalizing state of being and I got some dubious respect. I will say that.

Reveille came and went and I could pretend no longer. I took Leftkovitz's chair behind a typewriter in the Orderly Room. In an adjacent room Lt. Culpepper, the Company Commander, sat. The Company Commander should have been a Captain, but through some twisting of the rules, Lt. Culpepper had taken the role because maybe, due to reduced ranks after World War II ended, there not enough Captains to go around. Perhaps he was serving his time out for discharge and the army did with him, as it did with all of us, as it pleased. Lt. Culpepper was short, plump, and sported the flushed cheeks of an alcoholic. One got the feeling after five seconds in his presence that he didn't much care for the army. He was looking to put in his 20 years or so and then a pension and a retirement and to forget all about it. Like the First Sergeant, like many, he had served through World War II, but where I never learned. Officers didn't share life facts with enlisted men. Once it rained, a driving pelting onslaught over the country side. Seated in my Company Clerk's chair, I said, "Water, water everywhere and not a drop to drink." I said it to show that I came from where language was prized, where learning was a benefit for the few, and that, lest we forget, I was hot shit. From the room with the door half closed I heard Lt. Culpepper's rising voice in recitation:

Water, water, everywhere,
And all the boards did shrink,
Water, water, everywhere,
Nor any drop to drink.

In his regular voice: "It's NOT *not a drop to drink;* it's *nor any drop to drink!* What do they teach you in that broken down high school you went to?"

I never tried any scholarship on him again but I never stopped trying to figure him out. He had an abiding hatred for one Major Lucey. Major Lucey was in charge of MP's who patrolled Seoul, they on the outlook for whore hopping, public drunkenness and fisticuffs. I carried the natural wariness in regard to Lucey and his roving Gestapo team but figured it was just part of the way the army did business and there was nothing to do about it. Just go on with life when on a pass in Seoul and don't let paranoia ruin any fun. And so one evening I was rounded up in an Off-Limits dance hall on Bung Chung Street along with many in our Company. When the names were presented to Lt. Lee in the Orderly Room for discipline, he screamed, "That fucking cocksucker Lucey, the cunt. Hasn't he got anything better to do!" Men who had been caught, though, were disciplined by Culpepper. He had to do it: No passes for a while, KP duty, third or fourth offense and off to the stockade. But was Culpepper mad! He kept cursing Lucey and his cursing was spectacular even by army standards that had made cursing a high art form. My turn came to face Lt. Culpepper with the door shut. I thought I would get off with a wink and a nod and a slight reprimand. After all I was on his team in the Orderly Room through the day, stationed behind a desk a few feet from him. I had come close to quoting Coleridge correctly. We would just go through the motions I was sure. I was a foot taller than he was. "Shut the door," he said. Then: "Bowers, stand at attention! You are in an officer's presence. Where's the fucking salute?"

He got the salute and I stared straight ahead and not at him. I couldn't get it out of my mind, though, that he was a First Lieutenant when a Company Commander was supposed to be a Captain.

"What do you mean going in a dance hall that was clearly marked Off Limits! What kind of fool are you? Can't you read?"

"But everyone else …"

"Fuck everyone else."

I pulled out my ace in the hole. "But Major Lucey just picked me out for no good reason I know of. Maybe a girl turned him down there."

The look I got back froze me. Lt. Culpepper's cheeks flamed. "Major Lacey was doing his job. He's an officer in the U.S. Army. You will not get a pass for a month. You understand!"

"*Yes, sir!*"

"*Dismissed!*"

Sergeant Weldon was leaning back in his chair as I walked a few feet to my desk. He gave me a thin smile.

Sergeant Weldon before he got downsized at World War II's end had of course been a Captain. He had led men through the Argonne and now he demurred slightly when he had to to First Lieutenant Culpepper. He did not do any more demurring than was necessary. Other officers who didn't measure up to his standards, no matter what rank, got short shrift I soon found out. One was Captain Pitt, a Battalion doctor. Captain Pitt, the MD, was a Pretty Boy who felt privileged by his medical status and his Farley Granger good looks. I encountered his likes later in life, over and over. He was the kind of doctor who makes you wait in the outer office for over an hour even though he may not be seeing another patient, just to show his importance, or is taking his sweet time with a favored one. He is lazy. He shows his profile and wallows in admiration. He expects bows, not reprimands. The men in Company C were having trouble once seeing Captain Pitt when they turned up on Sick Call. They were told to wait, to go back on duty and see if whatever ailed them went away. It was warm weather then and Sergeant Weldon caught Captain Pitt sunbathing in a bikini on the roof of an old Japanese building. He marched up to him.

"My men are lined up waiting to see you," he announced. He didn't call him, Sir. He didn't address him as, Captain. He held contempt in narrow Texan eyes.

"Thank you for the information, Sergeant. Tell them I'll be down after a while."

"I won't tell them a God damn fucking thing. You get your sorry fucking ass down there and treat my men. I mean right now."

I had followed behind. I saw the self-satisfied look in the Captain's eyes dim. I saw a frightened confused man. "I got to –"

"You got to get your fucking ass down there in five seconds or I'm throwing you off this roof."

He was down there in two seconds, buttoning his shirt, stethoscope jiggling.

And then there was Second Lieutenant Pulley, a recent West Point grad. Lt. Pulley had bright green eyes and a serious, let's-get-to-business look, don't waste my time. He was friendly with the troops but not familiar. He did not inquire about any one's background or interests and of course neither did we about him. He wore a West Point class ring and his uniform was neat and clean and the gold bars on his collar seemed to glisten extra strong. But the lasting image I have of Lt. Pulley was with his head poking through a slick poncho where drops of water clung. It was the rainy season and Lt. Pulley burst into the Orderly Room in late evening where Sgt. Weldon was ambling around and I was putting together the guard roster for the next day. Sgt. Weldon had had a few under his belt as he had most evenings. His breath carried far. "Sergeant," Lt. Pulley said, "the road a few miles up is in danger of being washed away. Just been up there on re-con. We need sand bags and gravel to secure it. Let's get a detail up there right away."

Sgt. Weldon took his time. He looked out the window at the sheets of rain that were coming down and near shaking the building. "Why not wait until morning when we have light to see what we're doing, Lieutenant? We could lose someone out there in this."

I saw disbelief in the lieutenant's face. He had given an order that was in danger of being disobeyed. What to do? He glanced ever so slightly my way to perhaps get some help. He was looking the wrong way. I had nothing against the lieutenant but I was under the employment of Sgt. Weldon. I was out of it but I was a witness and I could see that the lieutenant feared losing face. On the other hand Sgt. Weldon was in danger, strictly speaking, of a General Court Marshal.

Lt. Pulley began throwing out engineering terms and spoke of the curving, seldom used little road as if it was the gateway to Berlin in the Second World War; he spoke again of sand bags and gravel, sand bags and gravel, and ended by ordering the sergeant to put a detail out in the lashing rain. I had never seen such rain as the rain that night in Korea. It was right up there with the cold in the cold season.

"I'm not going to lose any of my men in this weather tonight, Lieutenant. It's not necessary." He didn't say, "Sir." "Morning and daylight is soon enough." As he spoke near the side of my face his breath nearly knocked me over.

Lt. Pulley paused. I visualized the Spring Hop, or whatever they had up there at West Point, girls in evening gowns, cadets with sabers raised or whatever; the tidy rooms and endless study and the endless drills and marching on the Plains in perfect formations. There was four years of it. It was where U.S. Grant, Sherman and Ike had passed through, not to mention George S. Patton. Lt. Pulley glanced again my way and I, in embarrassment and some fear, looked down. "O.K., if that's how you feel," Lt. Pulley said in a huff and marched in his wet poncho out the door of the Orderly Room, not to return that evening. No one came to take Sgt. Weldon away. He pulled a bottle from his desk, took a pull on it, put it back, winked at me and left. The rain lessened the next day into a gray drizzly one, and Sgt. Weldon sent out a detail to shore up the road. They came back muddy, in pride at getting a tough job done, and in silence. Lt. Pulley acted as if any confrontation had never taken place, as if his orders had been carried out to the letter the night before. But he avoided my eyes in the Orderly Room. He avoided Sgt. Weldon as best he could.

* * *

At first, when I had taken on the reigns of Company Clerk, Leftkovitz on the high seas off for home, I myself gave Sgt. Weldon a wide berth. He was the Top Kick, he had fought in Europe, he ran the Company while Company

Commander Culpepper remained largely behind his half-closed door, occasionally screaming out a malediction against something or someone. For some reason Culpepper had an abiding hatred of the late President, Franklin D. Roosevelt, whom my father believed could have walked on water. Lt. Culpepper was reading something that had come through the mail when suddenly from his lair came: "That son of bitch sold the country down the river! Can't America understand that fact, God damn it!" I thought I was listening to some crackpot Republican back home whom I thought I'd left far behind. But Culpepper surprised me. He had equal fixation and distaste for General Douglas MacArthur whom he referred to as "Dugout Doug." "Ever see that shot of Dugout Doug wading ashore in the Philippines?" he once whispered conspiratorially in my ear, leaning over while I sat at my desk, causing me to jump. "All staged. All set up. They should stick that corncob pipe up his ass." And walked off.

I can't remember his ever talking to Sgt. Weldon. They did not show a discomfort or dislike toward one another but something stopped communication. Lt. Culpepper was in command of the Company and roused himself forcefully in the role of authority when necessary but left day to day matters in the hands of Sgt. Weldon. At that time, maybe now, officers were in a world far removed from the rabble. Sgt. Weldon had once been an officer, whether comfortably or not I couldn't say. But he never bad mouthed, or took after, an officer simply because he was an officer. I figured since he had been an officer himself once there was nothing mysterious about being one. It was a mystery though to me and many others. I pictured officer housing and the officer mess as removed from the normal form of existence. There would be a table cloth and gleaming silver and a mess Stewart, a GI, to serve them – steak probably and bread in a basket. The dinner chat would be interesting and perhaps there'd be a bit of wine to go with the steak. They slept in rooms, not in rows as we did in the barracks where snoring rattled the windows and no easy chairs or reading lights existed. If you were in the service at an early age, at 18 or 19, an enlisted man, you would never forget the distinction, good and bad, that someone's having been an officer carried, no matter how high up in civilian life you went. James Jones and Norman Mailer, the chroniclers of World War II, never forgot. When they found out someone had been an officer their attitude changed in the glint of an eye, hardly ever for the good.

Being an Enlisted Man and having some years and a little heft on you usually provided a better perspective with an added dollop of cunning to get through service days and out of it. Once I helped a corporal named Willoch repair the furnace at the Officers' Quarters. (Yes, a furnace when the ranks made do with a pot-bellied stove.) Why I was chosen to help him I can't remember, but chosen I was, probably because no one else was available. Willoch had been a plumber in civilian life and was unlucky enough to have been drafted, ending up in Korea. He had a quiet way of speaking with a wary eye that told you he was on to you, that your bull shit didn't go far with him. He loathed the army and the fact that he was in it, especially since he was married and it had separated him from hearth and home. He'd been minding his own business, happy with his wife, no children for distraction, when his draft letter came and now he was half way around the world, off to fix a furnace for a dumb privileged few. We talked as we navigated our way on a path between rice paddies, woozy from the smell of garlic and honey carts that lay like a vapor over the land. Oh, Lord, please get me home! Willoch spoke of the low intelligence of officers, mixed with outrage at their pampered lives. I envied them but had no outrage. I kept imagining myself as one.

At a small lean-to attached to a larger, low-slung structure was the furnace room of the Officers Quarters. It was chilly and no sound came from what I took to be a furnace, a small motor and a tin contraption with some dials and switches on it. Willoch opened a well used canvas satchel he'd been carrying and brought out a screw driver.

"I thought you were a plumber," I said.

"The army fucks everything up. They think plumbers and electricians are the same. Actually I do know something about electricity. Not much, but something. Let's just hope we don't blow ourselves up. Anyhow, we've got the afternoon off. I'm in no hurry to get back."

Willoch looked like he knew what he was doing. He moved a wire here, tapped a gadget there. He used wrench, hammer and screw driver. He then stood back, drank in the whole shebang, scratched his chin, and threw the switch. The motor rumbled, caught, and began a steady purr. A look of pleasure mixed with apprehension drifted across his face. The machine might sputter out, but didn't. Much much later in life, when I was in a different income bracket, a householder, I witnessed this look on a worker's face after he had solved a riddle and made a complicated water faucet behave after I had failed. He was a professional; Willoch was too, and a working man. Willoch might hate officers and wish them all frozen to death, but he had conquered the machine that gave them heat. "I'm going to wash up," he said.

He left the furnace room and marched into the Officers' Quarters and Mess as if he owned them. He came out with his oil-stained bag bulging more than when he entered. He held his back ramrod straight and his head high. On the walk back through the rice paddy he stopped and opened the bag. I forget what he brought out but it was something to eat and something to drink. I marveled at his skill at theft but turned down his offer of a taste and sip. We were never teamed up again. I became a Company Clerk, promoted to a T/Four, and Willoch went back to the States to his wife.

* * *

I then had Sgt. Weldon in my life for the rest of my tour in Korea. He was starting to have a little flab under his chin and his waist molded in with his ample hips. At first he was, or tried to be, gruff with me as he was with most who passed his way. I was, or tried to be, attentive to what a good soldier should be. I sat up straight in my chair before the typewriter with sheaves of paper around me. There was a Somerset Maugham novel in there somewhere. He spied it, picked it up as if it might bruise, studied the cover, flipped it open, and scanned a line or two. "You like this stuff?" he said.

"He's a pretty good story teller but I don't think it's literature."

"I don't read much." He about-faced and took a seat at his desk. I could tell he was thinking. "My wife back in Texas reads a lot. I just let her alone with that. And she lets me alone with some of the things I do."

"What's that?"

"Oh…" He thought some more. I feared he might not come up with anything and then be angry. He said, with a touch of embarrassment, "Oh…well…I do a little woodworking." He thought some more. "But…well, you know, that's a crock of shit when you come down to it. I generally just sit down in the basement thinking that I should be woodworking. You want to know something else?"

"Yeah. Sure."

"I haven't been home that much with my wife in the time we've been married. There was the war, you know, and then Stateside service and now, here I am a million miles away. It's piss pot awful, son."

"Why don't you get out? You've served your time."

I could tell we both had the same thought at that moment. Should he be talking this way, revealing this much? He was Top Kick of the Company. He had fought, probably bare-handed, the Germans. He scared everyone, officers and men alike in the Company. He collected himself with a shake of his shoulders and brought his hands down on his desk. "I don't want a discharge. I could never hack it on the outside. You want to know what I do? I soldier, son. I'm a fucking soldier. That's what I do."

I was a Company Clerk. That's what I now did. I cared not that I had it relatively easy, no guard duty and no KP. I had served my time on the line, been burned out of quarters, been half-frozen on Guard, and had no qualms about a soft berth. The time of seeking adventure and new experiences had vanished from my agenda. I sought to put in my time, as one would in prison, and then get the hell out of a place I figured I had no business being in, Korea. My cot was in a room right outside the Orderly Room. Sgt. Weldon was there, too, in the first cot, with a large private space and immediate access to the Orderly Room, the hub of operations. Sometimes he would stay in the Orderly Room long after lights out, doing what I wasn't sure.

One night I found out what he'd been doing. He'd been drinking, all by himself, at his desk. He came in the sleeping quarters and shook my shoulders. "Get up," he barked, and added, "please. If you don't mind."

I was structured to do whatever this man said. I rolled out of a dream I was having about Tennessee, pulled on my fatigues, and followed him into the Orderly Room. Lights blazed. On his desk lay several crumpled up pieces of paper. There was a fountain pen, cap off, beside a clean sheet. Next to it was half drunk bottle of Seven Crown. "Sit down," he said. I did so, in his chair. "Now I'm trying to put into words what I feel about my wife and I want her to know it. I got feelings but the words don't come out right. I want you to do it for me. That should be a simple enough thing to do."

"O.K.," I said, reaching for the pen. "I'll try."

"No, type it and I'll write it up later in my own handwriting if I approve of what you've done." I hauled the battered Royal over, the one on which I typed out every day the guard roster and those up for KP and rolled in a clean sheet. My hands hovered over the keyboard like a pianist. "Dear Merrita," he began.

"What kind of name is that? How do you spell it?"

"Just type, God damn it! It was the name she was born with. Spell it any way you like. Dear Merrita," he continued, "I'm thinking of you back in Texas, probably laying on your back looking up at the ceiling and wishing I was there looking down on you…Well, I… No, that's not it! Put it better words, you know what I'm getting at, I miss her, that sort of shit, you'll know what to do. "

"Go on."

"Merrita," he dictated, "wives are coming over here to join their husbands. Yeah, the Army's doing that for us. Our Company Commander's wife will be here any day, the army's doing that, it's true. He's a Looie. Was a Major but came down to stay in and work toward a pension. Like me, coming down from a Captain. Officer wives are coming over now but I hear it's non-commissioned wives next. You'll come. We'll see all the sights together and bring home souvenirs. I'm thinking of you, honey, laying there on your back. Make it nice," he said to me, leaning over, his breath heavy with alcohol, his eyes bloodshot and nearly bleeding. "Type it up."

I did so and he liked what he saw or he said so, moving his lips while he read. I was thinking of the girl I'd never kissed in Tennessee while I wrote. I threw in all my longing for home and what I thought was the better angels of my nature. "That's some shit," he said. "She's going to think

I've gone mad. I just hope she's not fucking someone else now."

I did other letters for him as time went on. The weather now was hot and he would come to my bunk, shake my shoulder, and motion for me to follow him into the Orderly Room. fumes of booze left behind in his wake. I tagged along in my GI issue Olive Drab draw string drawers that came down to the top of my knees and ballooned in the ass, taking my usual seat, fingers over the keyboard. He wrote to a home mortgage company about a late payment, to an elderly uncle about a major league baseball team, and to a comrade from the battle of the Bulge. "Whitey, you won't believe this place," he dictated, in a message to the former army buddy. "It sure ain't what we went through but worse in some ways. It's that you got to live, night and day, with the feeling that we ended it once and now here we are waiting for it happen again. There are sons a bitches up there above us, the Russians or gooks or whoever the fuck they are I don't know, champing at the bit to come down on us. I understand the fucking Krauts. They looked more like us than we do ourselves and they fought in a hard ass but regular way, but this new bunch I don't know what to say. All I want is to be back home sitting on the porch, scratching my balls and waiting for the sun to set. Type that up in better English, son."

I never learned who Whitey was, what rank he had been and what had happened to him and the Sergeant in the War. Sgt. Weldon didn't give out too much information, but certain things I came to understand.

Sgt. Weldon had no children. I figured he hadn't been back in the States long enough, what with World War II and now Korea, to father one. I was pleased when he began to treat me in a fatherly and older brother way but I already had a father and an older brother and they were as much as I could handle. I ceased being in abject fear of him but knew enough to give him respect and watch out and not trigger his temper. He genuinely liked me I felt and I wanted to do a good job and try to do what I could to keep him out of trouble. I might have made a pretty good adjutant if I'd stayed on in the army and got into officer territory but that would never be. "Don't be like me, son. Don't ever make a career of this," he told me more than once. He didn't have to tell me. I was counting the days.

It was pretty cozy not having to pull guard duty or KP or go out on the line but it didn't pay to get too comfortable. The unexpected had a way of happening. One night, shortly after lights out, while I was drifting off, a soldier burst in to stand beside the netting over Sgt. Weldon's bunk. Mosquitoes were in season. "Sergeant, that Jew is missing. He didn't show up for guard."

"What's that, what are you talking about?"

"Jew is missing. I can't find him anywhere. We need somebody to take his place on post."

"Bowers," Sgt. Weldon called down from his superior perch at the front berth, after cursing for awhile, "take care of this for me, will you?"

This involved Pvt. Yuan Jew, a dreamy, child-like, perpetually smiling creature who had "Jew" as a last name. It was spelled that way and pronounced that way. He was Chinese to the core and far from Hebraic persuasion. We all came from diverse backgrounds, touchy about one thing or another, Americans all, and no one wanted to deal with his name the wrong way. You feared being tainted with prejudice where all of us were, as nowhere else, in a melting pot of origin and belief. I always tried to say "Jew" casually as if it carried no freight, as if I was speaking to someone named "Jones." If you hooted or made a sly comment then you might be suspected, or nailed, for anti-Semitism. The worst. Best to just go on with it. Forget about it. "God damn that Jew," I said. "Now I got to pull it."

"Thanks, John," Sgt. Weldon called down. "Good soldier. Appreciate it."

By assigning me to fix it Sgt. Weldon wouldn't have to roll out of his bunk and investigate and make charges against Pvt. Jew. I went out on guard and nothing happened. I sat in the guard tower, thought about biscuits and gravy and the girl I had never kissed, and at the end climbed aboard a two-and-a-half as day broke and relief came. Nothing happened to Pvt. Jew. He showed up dreamily from some place for Reveille, showed up as if it was the most natural thing in the world to miss guard duty – what was the big deal? – and he was never questioned about where he had spent the night, nothing. It would have been too much trouble, too much paperwork and aggravation to go further with it. He never tried it again. I don't know what Sgt. Weldon said to him.

*   *   *

The battalion moved once more, to a compound near Seoul that only a couple of years before the Japanese had used as a school. We slept in classrooms where the walls were thick and the floor didn't creak. Those occupiers had apparently felt that the school would be there for a millennium as the Germans about the Third Reich. No one saw Hiroshima coming, no one saw the Rising Sun falling. Occupiers nearly always get the tables turned on them. Occupying some place one moment, being occupied themselves the next. Occupying someone else's land would no longer be an option for those of the Rising Sun. And here in their once secure compound we now watched films in an auditorium where the Stars and Stripes rose on a stanchion to the side, Cary Grant and Ingrid Bergman's big heads illuminated on a screen, and where a few USO entertainers trotted in to perform on stage.

TKI have an old Kodak snapshot of a leggy young woman in tan slacks, with a wasp waist and a cute butt, squinting her eyes, chin tucked, looking quizzically at the camera. It was taken in bright sunshine. Every time I look at it, pulling it out of long storage, I am struck by two things. First, that I stand there beside her, not touching, but there. Number two, that she resembles the girl I never kissed from Tennessee. Mementoes from the past cannot bring all of it back, all that went into that moment and day. She must have been only a year or two, if that, older than me. She was a show girl. God, how I love the sound of that name even now. Show girl! And I could count on the fingers of one hand the Stateside women I encountered in Korea. This one was one. How I got beside her for the shot I don't know. I remember that I couldn't progress further with her than a nod and a smile and a request from someone that we stand beside each other for the shot from a Kodak camera. I do remember – and am I kidding myself? – that she expected something more from me than just a camera shot. Could it be she had wanted to tell me where she came from in the States, what her career plans were, what her family was like? She steps right out of the 1940's with her hairdo and slacks but the rest is a blank. I should perhaps have invited her out for a soda – if there had been the improbability of a soda fountain in the Mountain Kingdom – but I was 18 and had yet to acquire any pick-up skills, only embarrassment. Probably she went on to marriage, kids, disappointments and what not, but we do have this split second in the sun, forever recorded. She appears expectant. I stand, for a reason that escapes me, cocksure.

Other snapshots surface in a green silk photo album that is falling apart. There are shots of young Korean boys that acted as go-fers for us. They took bundles of our clothes out for washing and ironing. They swept the place. They giggled and took in good humor our ribbing and faux stances of superiority and power. We communicated in pidgin English and the miniscule Korean we had learned, mainly of the crass variety. At the drop of a hat they would figure out a way to provide a service or some goods that would lead to some funny money or cigarettes going their way. Already, at an age when manhood was a shadow away, they had become shrewd in business. You want it, Joe? We get it for you, chop chop. Childhood had been missed. We never stepped in a Korean home on a social visit. We really didn't know who they were. With our own troubles, we didn't care to know. We were Occupiers, that was all we knew.

I now think of an older youth, one in his late teens or early 20's who descended on us one afternoon with an ingratiating smile and an armload of goods and services like a Civil War sutter on the heels of the troops. How he got in our compound past a guard I do not know. He had silk scarves to unload and the services of a jack of all trades artist, who could copy in a drawing and enlarge, in color, what passed as a portrait from a figure in a snapshot. Today, hanging on the wall in a Catskills cabin, is a portrait of my father who looks as stately as a judge with rosy cheeks and pompadour hair, originally snow white, now the color of a canary. The youth in our quarters had the mein of a middle-age man. He smiled, nodded, and became very serious and obsequious. If we passed on something he quickly moved on, slyly returning to what we had turned down seconds before. He liked to be paid in cigarettes but could barter and even deal in credit. Pay me next time, Joe, I trust you. When he humbly walked away, shoulders lowered, I noted a large patch sewn on his rear end. He was impoverished but I bet before long would make out like a bandit. The Mountain Kingdom produced the shrewd and enterprising.

Decades later, after many roles had been played, many sights seen, age hanging over me like a shroud, I walk into one of the small, clean, prosperous Korean groceries that dot the landscape of New York. They've just sprung up, all neat and well lit and having what you need in an emergency, milk or toilet paper, something like that. It's late or a holiday, and regular outlets have had the good sense to close and enjoy life, but these Koreans are open to all comers. At the register, holding the necessary goods – overly priced because they can get away with it and are justified in doing so – I fight the impulse to let loose with some dirty Korean. What a crazy thought. Just let loose out of the blue with words for sexual intercourse and organs. What would they say? What would that pretty, sloe-eyed Korean girl say, adding up the bill? I'm deathly afraid of that impulse. It's a legacy from service to my country.

Long ago in Korea I slept in one bunk after another, in place after place, our battalion inexorably moving about the countryside like gypsies. We didn't do anything new with each move, we just moved. In the lower ranks, of which I was one, we didn't know why or particularly care. It could have been our dubious engineering skills, which essentially called for keeping an eye on Korean laborers, who did whatever roadwork or construction was called for. We moved, maybe to keep the North Koreans and Soviets guessing, maybe to give us something to do. If you're in the Army you are not told why things are done. Each move meant someone new took a bunk beside you. On a late sunshiny day a soldier named Anderson from Missouri, fresh from the States, threw his duffle bag on the bunk next to mine. He was lanky and unsmiling, dour, a fine representative of the "show me" state. We should have got along, and we did for awhile, because he came from a small rural town as I did. Missouri and Tennessee were not that far apart. We traded stories about our recent high school days. Nothing much had happened to him, I gathered.

At the time I was writing away for college applications. I was going to put the GI Bill to use. Yes, sir. So they came – colorful catalogues, questionnaires, the elite names of universities in bold letters. Hell, you could apply anywhere.

As a GI you didn't even have to pay postage. On my bunk after mail call I brought out the academic paraphernalia and spread it out like a deck of cards. I was a little shy about bringing it out, but only a little. I thought secretly that I might get a notch up in esteem if someone spied these college brochures and application forms. Anderson had the habit, possibly from his "Show Me State" background of turning over objects and examining whatever lay near. He'd pick up your M-1, pull it up, and look down the muzzle. He'd flip over a V-Mail letter you left on your locker, looking to see who sent it. It was a compulsion. He didn't know better, I figured. He picked up one of the applications and felt it between his fingers as if the quality of the paper would tell him something. "You going there? Harvard?"

"I don't know. It's just an application."

"Some shit," he said, and tossed it back on the bunk.

We didn't get into a fight that day. When we did, it didn't start as a fight. It began as horseplay. One late afternoon, as we were kidding around over something, he just happened to punch my shoulder. As we stood between our bunks he hit my shoulder. It wasn't hard, but who gave him permission? I pushed him back, hard. He grabbed me suddenly around the neck in a half nelson, and I wrestled him over a bunk. And before we knew it, we had committed ourselves to a full fledged fight without any words being spoken. We wrestled and tugged at each other and knocked against any who stood in our way. It was exhilarating. We let loose with grunts and punches, letting it all out. I hadn't been in a fight since grammar school. "Stop 'em, grab 'em!" someone screamed. Before anyone could we fell against the stove, which wasn't lit, and knocked it over. We knocked over a poker game. We fought until we could fight no more, a crowd gathered around us. After a final weak jab or two we just quit in mid-punch. No one had started it, no one ended it. No one said anything. My right eye was swelling and my knees were buckling. We went our separate ways. What the hell was that? I never felt better in my life.

* * *

The army owned you. I learned that soon enough. It could wake you up in the morning, send you to bed at night. It gave you food to eat. It sent you out on guard duty and told you to pull KP. It wasn't exactly a democratic organization. Back home I had a habit of suddenly taking off for a walk downtown, asking no one's permission, following a path of my own – down Boone Street, across Market, up Roan, across Watauga, back home. I could do that any time I liked and I had been doing it six or so months before. Now I was halfway around the world needing a pass to get outside the gates. A boy I knew only by sight in the outfit decided he didn't want to pull Guard one evening. His name was on the board, he was due to report for inspection. But he'd had enough apparently. He sat on his bunk not moving a muscle, his face blank. He just didn't want to do it. A squad leader began yelling at him. "It's your turn, God damn it! Get your ass out there! What do you think you're doing!"

He got up, but instead of moving out, joined a crap game going on in the corner. It was as if he'd lost his hearing. Later in life I read Melville's "Bartleby the Scribbiner" and remembered that soldier's face when he said he just wasn't going to do it. The squad leader walked off in a huff.

The dice game went on. The soldier won some, lost some, remained in the game with the same blank expression on his face. Suddenly the squad leader returned. Behind him came Sergeant Weldon walking slowly, expressionless, and determined. Sergeant Weldon stood over the dice game, saying nothing for awhile. Then he said, not in his normal bark, but rather softly, "I hear you're not going out on Guard. Is this correct? Anything troubling you?"

The boy said nothing. The dice stopping rolling. All eyes turned on him. He blushed. Sergeant Weldon stood over him. Then he said, again softly, "better get out there, son. The truck's about to leave."

The boy, whose turn it was to shoot the dice, stood, didn't look at Sgt. Weldon and walked out for Guard duty.

* * *

We moved, we kept moving. In tropical heat I moved into a room off the Orderly Room. I had a new roommate at that juncture: Red the Mailman. His cheeks were full and preternaturally red, a shade darker than the hair on his head. He was a big lumbering boy who took ten minutes to do a two minute task. I was from the South but could forget about it for stretches, especially if no one brought it up and imitated my twang. Red you could never lose sight of his Southerness in all its stereotypes. He oozed laziness and diffidence. He hardly ever cracked a smile but whatever he said or did came out funny.

We put up mosquito netting around our bunks in the hot months although I can't remember many, if any, mosquitoes in Korea. Maybe I wasn't on the outlook for them. But orders were orders and who knew who or what was going to attack us? We had shots for cholera and Bubonic plague. One shot we all got jabbed with, it could have been the one to ward off the Bubonic plague, caused a purple knot the size of a goose egg to swell on your arm. We all went around comparing our knots, awed by them and in competition to see who had the largest one.

In our two-man cubby-hole room Red snored. He snored operatically with deep explosions of breath that made his lips flutter and him coming awake with a start at times. At first I was mad at his snoring, felt put upon because I had to endure it at close quarters. The bunks weren't that far apart and often when Red was really into it I would reach a foot over and shake his bunk It worked one or two times and then he was back to sawing wood as if nothing had happened. That made me mad, too.

Another maddening thing was that he liked to sleep with a light on. I never heard of such a thing and had little sympathy. If I complained he drawled out that he would turn it off, don't worry about it. He never did. Among our privileges in the little room was that we didn't we didn't have to follow barracks rules about lights out. When I determined that he was asleep, usually at the first deep rumble of a snore, I got up and pulled the chain on the overhead, naked bulb. Once I lay there, waiting, sleepless, the light on and I saw his hand reach out and fling the netting aside. he jumped out of his bunk, stood up straight, and shouted, "Take that, you fly smasher!" Then he flung back the netting and climbed back in bed and began snoring.

I didn't know what to make of that, but kept thinking about it. Was Red a sleep walker like Lady Macbeth? Would he the next time walk out of the room and out into the night? What if combat came and he sleep-walked out of a foxhole into the arms of the enemy? What finally got me was what he meant by "fly smasher." What was he talking about? It was among a myriad of things I never found an answer to in the army. There was the roughneck boy from, I hate say it, again from the South, from the swamplands of Florida. In basic training at Fort Knox, while the rest of us were in Louisville on weekend passes, he moved all bunks and lockers except his own against a wall. He was uncommonly strong. Then he poured lighter fluid around it and tossed in a match. Scuttlebutt had it that he went to bed while flames rose. No one found a definite answer for why he did it. They said he might have been drunk and mad that he had been denied a pass, but that was as far as it went. A fellow soldier passing by caught it just in time and doused it with buckets of water. Nothing was done to the soldier who set the fire.

Higher ups may have determined they needed someone like him in the ranks, a real roughneck. I remember him as hulking boy with the deadpan sleepy glaze of a killer. He'd had encounters with others from time to time and no one wanted to fight him.

Most of us young recruits at this time, hardly distinctive enough to call a band of brothers, had been conditioned by the big war that just ended. We had seen the movies, had seen our towns bursting with servicemen on leave or in transit, we had had big brothers come back with ribbons on their tunics. You didn't want to be left out. And wouldn't the glamour last forever? The uniforms, jitterbugging, the Andrew Sisters with their tits you were dreaming in there jiggling somewhere under their blouses, all set to bellow "The Bugle Call Rag"? What we didn't know was that it would end. The music would die. It was temporary, a chimera, and something else would grow from its embers and take its place and be considered permanent itself for awhile. Every generation, if you can call it that, makes its own world, to be toppled and made mincemeat by those that come afterward. Ah, if those who came back from stink and bombs and then put up a picket fence and settled down with a girl in white underwear thought they deserved a break they had another thing coming. What came was the 60's.

What came in 1946/47 was our occupying Korea right after the shooting stopped all over the world. Korea hadn't raised a gun against us. Korea had been occupied itself by the Japanese before we came to take over the South while the Soviets helped themselves to the North. World War II had ended and there was hardly a pause. And, when you come to think about it, we've been occupying, or trying to occupy, or making a mess of occupying, other countries and cultures ever since. Iraq is not isolated. And youth who bear the burden must continue to be youths who like to be reminded of their own culture back home. There was a Thanksgiving

Dinner where turkey and cranberry sauce suddenly materialized. There was, of all things, a tennis tournament. I had been on my high school tennis team back home and I immediately signed up. I would sign up for anything. I thought I might even have a shot at winning looking around at the talent in the Battalion. Actually there was no talent because I was the only one that volunteered. A jeep pulled up on a Saturday morning and I was introduced to an officer who was to shepherd me through the tournament. He was slim and nice looking and carried a happy innocent smile. He offered his hand and I shook it. I guess we had now left the officer/enlisted man world and had entered that of tennis and its refinements. I had been in the army long enough to feel uncomfortable around officers in a social situation and I had trouble not saluting. You didn't shake an officer's hand; you saluted and were put on guard to say the right, inoffensive thing. But tennis broke down class barrier. As he shifted the Jeep's gears he spoke about a player or two from different outfits and how happy he was that I would add competition. "Where was it you played?" he asked, in his happy tone.

"In high school," I said.

"What position?"

"I was number one," I said, but my conscience made me add, "There weren't that many who played tennis in the high school I went to."

"You'll do fine. Our battalion will be represented."

The wind and the roar of trucks along the pock-marked, unpaved road made conversation difficult, but to clarify certain points I had to make an effort. "I suppose they'll have racquets and tennis shoes where we're going, won't they?" I screamed

He seemed lost in thought for a moment. "They should," he screamed back.

We passed the usual: honey carts sloshing their goods as they rocked along, women with high stacks of straw on their shoulders, young barefoot boys laughing and screaming at us. By now I was used to the sharp aroma in the air that one never inhaled Stateside land and never forgot, of liquid human waste and garlic. Through it all the lieutenant and I drove and bounced in the Jeep to a tennis tournament. Two years hence mortar shells and machinegun fire would pierce the air and no laughing boys would line the roads. But today I was not thinking about that possibility but how to go to the net. I would send a ball cross court and then streak to that side and volley smartly the return to the other side. Net play. I had won matches in high school that way. I went over and over the movements, visualizing a shiny cup I would return to the battalion with. I was swift enough, and sly enough, I told myself.

We came to a fence behind which stood a sturdy concrete structure nestled in a clump of shade trees. Beside it was a tennis court, also concrete, and four or five rows of seats that rose for spectators. No one was playing. It was a sparklingly sunny day and a few soldiers were seated, talking among themselves. Most were officers. An enlisted man stood by the net of the concrete court holding a clipboard. It was a scene I'd witnessed several times in Tennessee when we'd played on clay courts that we watered and rolled and lay down fresh lines of white chalk on. "I'll just be a second," the lieutenant said. "Take a seat."

I took a seat and felt a familiar nervous thrill go through me. A match! Matches! My hands trembled. The lieutenant came back holding a pair of used, olive drab, high top basketball shoes. "Would you believe it? This is all they have for us. Just wanted to show you. Looks too big for you anyhow and I don't know what you'd do for shorts… Someone's fucked up big time!"

"That's O.K.," I said, trying to comfort him. I didn't want to leave. "Who's going to play?"

"Someone from the Seventh Army and someone from Intelligence. I've heard of that guy from the Seventh. He's pretty good. But," he glowered, "it really makes me mad. To get us out here, and no equipment or racquets. *That we were promised!*"

"What happened you think?"

"They claim we should have brought along our own. *Imagine!* They got indignant. *They* did! As if we carry tennis racquets and sporting gear around in our duffle bags. Someone's lying! They made it seem as if every size was available and they'd have every racquet on hand. You want to know the truth? I think someone's ripped off the supply room and they won't admit it now that we're here and they may be at fault. Could have been gooks. They'll steal the underwear right off you. Wouldn't surprise me to see tennis gear being sold right now on the side of the road."

Later, in reading accounts of war, it was not unusual to hear of promised artillery not being delivered, promised units not being sent, and essential equipment found missing. It brought back memories.

But how did the Seventh Army player come by his all whites and spiffy tennis racquet? Obviously not from GI issue and out of a duffle bag. His sponsors and superiors in the Seventh Army may have provided them. He was an asset they wanted to proclaim for whatever unbalanced reason. Or it all came shipped from home? Little mysteries trickle through the memories from Korea. For instance, what happened to the little boys, all innocent and giggly, who took our laundry for washing and ironing, and returned them neatly ironed? Boys, whose names we thought up to give them – such as "203" (called that, for whatever reason, another mystery), names we thought up because their real Korean names never came up. "203" was continually smiling, curious but never intrusive, on the job from dawn to dusk, seeking odd jobs and picking up English as he went along.

There was not a mean bone in his body. What happened to him when the firing began, when the bombs fell? Did he make it through? Could it be that now some Korean man who smiles and waits on me in a Korean deli in the Chelsea district of Manhattan is his grandson? Stranger things have happened. What we record in history books are the big things that often can't help being wrong or distorted, written by people who weren't there. Accepted history goes to the victor, as someone once pointed out. The extraordinary ordinary fades away with each generation. In ancient Rome there were undoubtedly countless characters known only in their neighborhood who had outstanding wit and unbelievable lives and whose tales ended with their deaths or shortly thereafter. There may have been a charmer who knew how slip in the Coliseum and sit in the Emperor's box undetected or maybe in the Emperor's lap. All lost, all gone.

And on the court this day, on the concrete court, I saw tennis I'd never seen before. The Seventh Army player, outfitted in all white, slashed balls left and right, bending his knees and following through. His serve was a blur. What would have happened to me if I had been unlucky enough to face him? It would have been an humiliation. He didn't give up a point. The match was over in no time. The small crowd gathered around him. The lieutenant stayed grumpily away and on the drive back said, "I bet you'd at least have got a point or two off him. I think he played for St. Mark's and is rated but you'd have found a way."

I'd never heard of St. Mark's or anyone being rated but I got a glimmer of another world out there of prep schools perhaps and athletics I knew nothing about. The lieutenant did. But I suspected that the lieutenant was incompetent and had got me out on a wild goose chase for a reason only he could answer. I suspected that the Army had never had a foolproof test for sanity and that the good lieutenant may have passed under the radar. The Army is a different place altogether. You become old at 18 or 19, and then you return home and are a kid again. But you hold a secret. It's often said that Vets do not like to talk about their experiences. They are kept from talking more because their experiences are so surreal and unlike anything in the civilian world that they wouldn't know where to begin. There is life in the Army, full of the unbelievable, and then there is life as a civilian. Different rules go into effect immediately when you cross over either way.

When I alighted from the Jeep in front of my barracks I saluted the lieutenant. I probably didn't have to because we had sort of broken down barriers, and I was surprised that I did it through reflex. He seemed surprised and his right hand made a brief flutter in the air. "Listen, next time I'll make sure we have equipment. You're the only player we have in the outfit. Don't want to lose you. There will be a next time!" He drove off. I never saw him again. But then our battalion did move around a lot.

But while we were stationary for a brief period an announcement went out again for volunteers. There was going to a talent night. A talent night! Anyone with comedic talents, operatic experience, play a musical instrument, or have some sort of talent we hadn't seen before and probably didn't suspect should sign up for talent night. It came to me that the Army wanted to continue the illusion that we were still at home, still had pleasantries happening, that sometimes we could feel we weren't in the Army and thousands of miles away from home at all. I had played the clarinet in Junior High but I would rather be shot dead than tootle away in front of the battalion. I had been on Amateur Night at the Tennessee Theater in Johnson City and had played without a screech "A Pocket Full of Miracles," which Bing Crosby had sung in the movies. The movies had enticed me to beg my mother for a clarinet in the first place. I had been fascinated by Benny Goodman letting it go on the licorice stick. I was no Benny Goodman and was hooted off the stage at Amateur Night. Let someone else make a fool of himself on Talent Night in Korea.

I must admit talent was more in evidence than I had expected. The MC was Lt. O'Leary, an unlikely West Pointer. It came out that his family, parents, grandfather, uncles and aunts had performed in Vaudeville and Burlesque. Why West Point then? Another mystery that stays with me. Maybe he wanted to break from family tradition. He was no Douglas MacArthur following in the footsteps of a Congressional Medal of Honor father. Maybe the family had sung so many patriotic songs on stage, like "Over There!" and "You're a Grand Old Flag", that they believed they owed one to the country. And the Congressman who guided his appointment through might have been a burlesque fan. Lt. O'Leary was chubby, good natured, and looked like an unmade bed – a shirt tail coming out, a belly, a bad shave, nothing pressed or shined. That's how he looked the night he stood before the mike in the old Japanese factory building that had been cleared of machinery but not the smell of oil, troops out in front of him, a ragtag band of Korean musicians behind him. What a relief it must have been to be back in the family business and enough of spit and polish. I was a little discombobulated, though, to see an officer, a West Pointer, suddenly turn into a burlesque comedian. He started off with a couple of really obscene jokes and then suddenly produced some colored balls from his baggy trousers and began juggling. The outfit went wild. The officers all loved Lt. O'Leary, you could tell. He probably entertained them in the Officers mess all the time. The men continued to be a little confused.

There was a swarthy, rather handsome youth from the Motor Pool who drove a two-and-a-half that took us to Seoul and to the field and to guard duty and who now took the mike in a graceful swipe of his hand. Actually he never seemed comfortable behind the wheel of a two-and-a-half as if his mind might be elsewhere, and he never entered into small talk. Now he looked up into a glaring light that hit him, waited for the musicians to strike some bars and then he began to a slow beat, in a soothing baritone that I for one never knew he had, *"Give me land, lots of land, under starry skies of blue… Don't fence me in…"* He wasn't bad, as I remember, but some in the audience began talking and there was one catcall that went something like, "Shove it up your ass, Marconi" that got a laugh but froze the smile on his face.

He came off the wobbly bandstand with the smile locked in place and then strode down the aisle and out the door. There must have been other acts that followed but they have been lost in the mist of time. I remember the Korean's band last piece, though, their closing number, as if they had just played it. I was captivated, stirred, but I had to return to the States to hear it again and learn its name. It was Rossini's "Overture to William Tell." [Light Cavalry Overture]. How had the Koreans come by it? The Army must have supplied sheet music and instruction. Surely the Japanese, whose Occupation had just ended hadn't had it their repertoire, although who knows? The band went at it on all cylinders, blasting away for dear life. I still can see a GI in the outfit, a slight soldier with glasses and pale skin, someone I'd never spoken a word to, who began beating a wooden stick of some sort against an empty chair, all in expert timing, eyes shut. Those of us not with a stick stomped our feet or clapped our hands in rhythm. We had got to Korea, the Koreans had survived the Japanese, the world was still turning! We'd get back home and goddam fuck everything!

The closer the time for the return trip came the more it crowded out all other thoughts and concerns. In my head I carried a mental picture of October. It was there the way the movies showed it on a calendar as images of months flipped by. I was in the Regular Army. No one had drafted me. The

Army and I had made a bargain. I would serve for a year and a half and then I would be discharged, no if's, and's or but's about it. I was in the volunteer Army, coming from the Volunteer state. Call us dumb but that's who we were: Volunteers. We were owned. In my case, on the heels of World War II, having a big brother who had been a Naval Officer, I had been seduced by the glamour of being in service, of wearing a uniform, of getting away from home, of proving my metal, of belonging. Oh, boy, that night after being sworn in at Camp McPherson and getting on the bus for Camp Oglethorpe in Georgia for assignment! The moon was out on June 28, 1946 lighting full bright the landscape and the curvy narrow road. I looked up at that moon and by God thought, I'm in the army. I'm a soldier! It's unbelievable. And a year later I was in Korea, counting the days as a year and a half drew nigh. Then a message from on ghih came down and I was one of the first to read it in the Orderly Room. A special excursion was available to any and all who wanted to visit China.

There was a caveat. The time taken on the junket, if such it was called, would be added to your enlistment. In other words, I would be delayed from from catching a ship home. I'd have to make up the days spent in sight seeing in China. A couple of weeks it would be, maybe longer. Maybe a Red army would descend during this time. Maybe I would miss the opportunity of getting back where I had started. Lawler, who had pronged his high school teacher, dropped by my bunk and there was no shilly-shallowing in his mind. He was going to China, you bethe was, even if it delayed him a month in getting back to the States. "A delay would be worth it," he said. "I'm going."

He went. Along with a few others from the battalion. They got to see old Shanghai, ride in rickshaws, go to nightclubs, and experience what was once China in its most international and decadent city. Two years later, after I was back in the States, going to fraternity parties and raising hell, Shanghai fell to Mao's army. No more sightseeing for GI's. But you have to give the Army credit for thinking up junkets and distractions like that. GI's got to take their minds off service duties and being stuck in a foreign hot spot and away from home, It was a harbinger of how our Occupations and endless wars would now include frills that others had not. Vietnam had its R & R's to Japan… Troopers bounced from Iraq and Afghanistan to home and back again to being encased in armored vehicles. They watched TV in Kabol and used text messaging and Skype to keep in touch with the folks back home. Stalingrad, Gettysburg, and Waterloo had more in common with the Peloponnesian War and the Siege of Troy than how war and Occupation played out. Now you have Drones where you pull the trigger without leaving home. Something must be wrong with that but we'll find out later, as we find out later things about the A-Bomb we know when we thought that up.

And wouldn't you know it? Lawler and the others didn't get their time shortened in leaving Korea by taking leave to go to Shanghai. Some miscalculation happened or someone thought it should just be given as a gift and less trouble to forget about it (more likely). I missed out and would have to wait over half a century to see Shanghai myself. It was not the same at age seventy-three as it would have been at 18. The thrill had gone along with the rickshaws.

But in Korea in 1948, now 19 and a T/4 and a company clerk, I could see the finish line as October and escape hove into view. I had served my enlistment. I was going home. But before that there was a celebratory party in the EM mess hall for those departing, complete with hard liquor and beer. Ranks mingled, officers in dress uniforms, EM's in suntans and ties. Some going, some celebrating our going and getting out of there, some staying. There stood captain Rothbart, not going, all spiffed up as usual, boots shined, hair trimmed, yapping away in his radio announcer's voice to a small cluster of EM's nervously gathered around him, EM's being able to mingle familiarly for once with an officer. I couldn't imagine what he might do in civilian life. I wondered that about many – Red the mailman, Red the Supply clerk, Red the drunk. What about Aberdeen? Would Lawler end up where he seemed to be heading, a solid citizen and family man who'd once porked his high school teacher? Daffy Duck was down in Pusan but was to catch the same ship home, the USS Admiral Mayo. Had he continued to correspond with the girl I had never kissed? Given the chance, he would drive me crazy.

We said goodbye to the Korean kids, innocents themselves, who did our laundry and made tidy our quarters and kept smiling through. Those were far more emotional moments than saying so long to fellow soldiers who, God help them, were still stuck in the Mountain Kingdom with no knowledge of what was soon to roll down from the North. There was one exception and totally unexpected in our farewells: Master Sergeant William Weldon, our Top Kick. My duffle bag stuffed with all I owned parked outside on the steps to the Orderly Room, I stood beside the desk where Sgt. Weldon sat, looking a little older, a little more tired than the day before. He stood and, whether an optical illusion or not, I thought his eyes were misting over. He smiled faintly. Here was a man who had received a battlefield commission, who had fought through France and Germany, and was now reduced in rank to get his pension, left behind in Korea. For what? Was he remembering the letters to his wife that I typed out? Was he thinking of how I went out in the middle of the night on Guard Duty when Jew took off? Was he thinking of how I stood beside him when he stood down the young West Pointer in the middle of a monsoon? Was I the innocent he once had been, the son he would never have?

Jesus, his eyes were misting over. "Be sure to write," he said. "Now get out of here."

He shook my hand; I pivoted an almost "about face" as the Army would have it and walked away. I passed the cracked-opened door to Lt. Lee's office. I spied him. He spied me. I gave a half-hearted wave of the hand, a near salute. He raised his right hand slightly, his face the customary crimson of a drunk, his eyes slits, I would never forget, no matter how many years later, his knowledge of Coleridge and his dressing me down for going in an "Off Limits" joint. We never had much to say to one another. Would he be there when the Reds came marching down. I picked up my crammed duffle bag and climbed aboard a two-and-a-half that bounced with two rows of soldiers to a waiting steam-engine train that would take us to the Admiral Mayo.

Heads sticking out the open train windows, fall air touched with a Korean flavor coming in, we passed the familiar sights: thatched huts, dusty roads, faces with timeless puzzled looks. Some of us hooted at the Koreans, and none too politely. We're getting out of here! So long suckers! They said or expressed nothing back. We passed by Kimpo air field and then the blue ocean suddenly rose, stretching out there and holding a big white ship. We had ended up in the harbor of Inchon where it had all begun, our Occupation of half the country. The ship was larger and seemed much sturdier than the Marine Dragon. It smelled a lot better. Our first meal was edible but there was no fresh milk or fruit. I still hadn't learned to drink coffee. I didn't care. I didn't care about anything except to find a bunk, not too high, not too low. Daffy Duck found me and let me know immediately that his first order of business when he got back was to take a train to see the girl of my dreams at her college in Georgia. How I dreamed of that all-girl college and girls in plaid skirts and her. Let him. Let him do anything. He made an exaggerated up and down movement and rolled left and right and the ship hadn't pulled out yet. When it did pull out and evening came, I ventured top side and looked up at the stars. The sea was calm with only small white capped waves around us. In the day the dice rolled in crap games in the hole and there was no nervous tension as there had been on the Marine Dragon. We had accomplished something in Korea although we didn't know what. I recognized several faces among those on board, officers and men, and any effect on me was now lost. I wasn't going to see many of them ever again. In most cases it was a comforting thought. No band of brothers here.

Day evolved into day into day until one morning on deck a seagull glided into view and alighted fluttering on a guard rail. That was a strange welcoming sight. There was a heavy soft fog, the ship's motor had lessened power to a low steady hum, and another seagull took a perch on the guardrail, and another – and then land! A port! We were back!

At Fort Lawton, outside Seattle, we began to process of disengaging ourselves from the U.S. Army – or re-enlisting. But first, a pass to go into Seattle! Somehow the atmosphere was subtly different than what it had been when we left San Francisco Bay with a band playing. It had been a little of over a year, now late 1947, the War over for over two years, a lifetime for public consciousness apparently. There were cold glances at our uniforms, not a beaming smile anywhere. We weren't special any more. More to the point , something might be wrong with us. In Seattle I found a dancehall and also found out that I could not order a beer because I was under 21. That was slightly upsetting because I was close to developing a taste for it. I didn't crave it, but I didn't think it right, just back from overseas, to be denied one. I danced, though, in the dancehall. A taffy-haired girl suddenly fell, for whatever reason, into my arms and I must have grown an inch or two in Korea because she seemed average height but my nose landed in her hair. I still decades and decades later remember the scent. It had just been shampooed with Brill. I could have left my nose there forever. Her breasts rubbed against my lower ribs. She did talk to me and at last there was a smile. Holding a girl in your arms in the 1940's to the lilt of a sentimental tune – say, "Goodnight, Sweetheart" or "I Want to get you on a Slow Boat to China" – allowed intimations into forbidden. You could rub against what you could get away with, but you didn't want to raise alarms by going into restricted areas too soon. It got complicated but you at least got to listen to music you could hum. And when a girl returned a slight thrust you got a thrill of a lifetime. The taffy-haired girl kept her distance and I thanked her for the dance. You did that back then.

Back at Fort Lawton the pace of getting a discharge was gone about slowly but surely. We listened to a nice-sounding Master Sergeant with ribbons galore speak about signing up for the Reserves and all the perks that would follow. "Men, you keep your rank. If, God forbid, a war breaks out, and that's highly unlikely, you go back in with your rank. What do you have to lose? Everybody will go back in if war comes." A lot signed up. It made sense in a way. Duffy Duck had somehow made Sergeant and he signed up. I had comparable rank but nothing on God's green earth could cause me to raise my right hand and join the Reserves. I had signed up once for the Army. That was enough. "You're crazy," Daffy informed me. "There's never going to be another war. Look what you get by being in the Reserves." In a couple of years war broke out in Korea. Daffy Duck went back to Korea.

At Fort Lawton we signed discharge papers, had a final short arm inspection, listened to a lecture or two, and that was it. We stood outside in the fresh air, on the quad, still feeling like soldiers, and heard a sergeant call,

"AttenSHUN!" We came to that stance as we were accustomed to doing for months on end, and the Sergeant said we would march outside to waiting buses to take us off base. "Let's keep it orderly!" He began, "FORWARD march! One, two, three, four …" We kept it up, marching as we were accustomed, duffle bags on our shoulders. Then a soldier in front of me began running. Another did. The Sergeant said to the first runner, "Get back in line, soldier!" The soldier, who was now an ex-soldier, looked over his shoulder, seeming not to know what to do. Finally he said, "I'm no more in the Army, Sarge! SO LONG!" And took off. We all began running, jumping up and down, the Sergeant yelling,. "HALT! HALT!" And we crowded on the bus amazed but delighted that we could break free while a sergeant with stripes on his sleeves and combat ribbons on his chest yelled for us to halt.

It was a long train trip back to Tennessee, cross country. As a perk we were accommodated to Pullman Sleeping Cars. In Kentucky, changing to another line to get home, no Pullmans granted, I bought a Saturday Evening Post, a Norman Rockwell painting of a happy America on the cover at a newstand. I lingered by the stand, drinking in the articles on the slick white paper, the heavy black print coming off on your fingers if rubbed. I drank in again the Norman Rockwell cover again, and then, magazine tucked under my arm, walked toward the waiting train. "Hey, there, you! You, soldier!"

I turned. I still wore my uniform. "Me?"

"Yes." It was a graying woman with a faint smile on her face. "Do you want to pay for that magazine?"

"I've already paid."

Her faint smile told me she was on to my game. She stood there patiently, waiting for me to reach in my pocket and pull out change. Maybe soldiers in transit had come through before, rowdy and thoughtless, or just perhaps people were tired of seeing uniforms and soldiers they perceived as expecting things without paying. Times had changed. But I had paid, I knew I had paid, and I wasn't going to pay again. I boarded the train with a brief glance back. The graying woman still stood there, the same faint smile on her face.

The deisel-engined train weaved past the hills and through the valleys in as I got closer to the home I had left in Tennessee. We stopped in towns I knew the names of like the back of my hand: Knoxville, Bull's Gap's where my father had once worked as a telegrapher. On and on, closer and closer... Did I need a shave? No, but I thought it best to be to be on the safe side and scrape off a scant bristle if I wanted a first-rate appearance for my homecoming. Wash rooms then on Southern Railway passenger trains had a distinctive aroma of grit and soap and abuse. Light came through an overhead fly-specked dome and from a narrow window as the train rocked along. The water was cold and I used hand soap but I managed to shave. And the towns came and went until... *Jonesborough!. . .* the small historic town where Andrew Jackson had once fought a duel. Next came, five miles away, the conductor bellowing it out, *Johnson City!* I had something like stage fright, my heart pumping in my chest, as I stumbled down the iron steps, duffle bag balanced on my shoulder, looking around for a familiar face. I first saw my pretty sister-in-law, as I remember, smiling. My father was home asleep because he worked third trick, the late night shift. My mother was there waving her handkerchief but had to hurry off because she now ran a book store and couldn't be absent for long. She gave me a distracted peck on the cheek and was gone. The train station had a section for "colored" and one for "whites," the water fountains equally marked.

At home my "room" was spiffily clean, my old clothes freshly washed and ironed and arranged neatly. I decided to wear my uniform and walked to the pool room as I used to do. No one looked up. It was great to be back home, but something kept bothering me. I wanted things to be different but also the same. It couldn't be done.

About the Author

John Bowers was raised in Johnson City, Tennessee, during the Great Depression and the World War II Era. After high school he enlisted in the US Armed Forces and was sent to Korea where he served for slightly over a year. On his return he took advantage of the G.I. bill, and went to the University of Tennessee from which he graduated in 1951. From there he went to the Handy Writers' Colony in Marshall, Illinois. His experience at the Writers' Colony became the basis of his acclaimed first memoir/novel, *The Colony*, which was published in 1971, nine years after he had moved to New York City.

During the 1960s and 1970s Bowers published numerous interviews and articles in *Playboy, Sports Illustrated, New York, Cosmopolitan* and *Harper's* as well as the *New York Times*. Among those profiled were Joe Namuth, Sharon Tate and Janice Joplin. Early in the 1980s he was commissioned to write a biography of Stonewall Jackson. *Stonewall Jackson: Portrait of a Soldier* was nominated for a Pulitzer prize.

John Bowers has taught creative non-fiction at the writing programs at Columbia and Wilkes Universities. He has two grown sons by his first marriage and four grandchildren. He is married to Leslie Armstrong, an architect and writer. They split their time between New York City and the Catskill Mountains.